AS YOU WANDER

100 DAYS OF DISCOVERING GOD WHEREVER YOU GO
BY KALEY RIVERA THOMPSON

Dear Wanderer,

To keep my ears from freezing off while living in Aspen, Colorado, I bought a beanie. In bold white letters, it had the word "WANDER" scripted across the front.

Wander means to roam or ramble with no real path or particular purpose. This word has defined my life and walk with God throughout my young adult years. A relentless desire to find him in unusual places has brought me here and everywhere I've ventured. It drove me across America, the whole world, and then to write this book.

"As You Wander" is a devotional inspired by many Jesus journeys and the lessons God has taught me along the unfixed path. Whether you're in the flatlands of Africa or on the tops of the great Rocky Mountains, at home or sitting in class, may you read, journal, or doodle and allow God to challenge you as seek him through your own wander years.

"As You Wander" is written for you. As a high school or college-age young woman, I wholeheartedly believe you can reverse the disconnection and faith deterioration in your generation. Here's why:

As a wife to a student pastor and someone who has been involved in student and worship ministry for years, I've heard the same thing over and over from young women. "Something has to change!" They're right, something does!

An epidemic of disconnection is sweeping through your generation. Young adults are leaving the church after high school at higher rates than ever before. College students report rising levels of depression, loneliness, and anxiety. School shootings and teen suicides rock our world.

But, here's the exciting part! The change bubbling under the surface is you: A tribe of young women empowered to be rebels with a cause.

You're tired of looking at people's social media highlight reels and want to get real. Instead of just commenting on people's pictures, you want to really care for your friends. You want to defy the odds, make a difference in your community, stand up for Christianity in your country, and get your hands dirty in the mission field. You really want to get out there and do all of these things. But, you don't know where to begin. That's why you're here.

You want a place to be courageously curious and a community to join you on the journey. "As You Wander" will help you see God in different ways, apply your faith practically, and help you understand God's Word. It's a space to ask hard questions and pull back the curtain on Christianity. It's for you, wherever you are on your spiritual journey and a safe place to process your purpose. It's a mentor who will never leave you, no matter where you may go.

This devotional book, along with our Instagram account (@asyouwandertribe), will be the very tools you need to join the Wander tribe and become the change in your generation. So, connect and let us help you process along your own unfixed path. Let's go, Wanderer!

This is "As You Wander" and this is for you.

Sincerely,
Kaley Rivera Thompson

As You Wander
100 Days of Discovering God Wherever You Go
by Kaley Rivera Thompson

Devotional Contents:

The saying not all who wander are lost is absolutely correct. It's in losing herself that a wanderer is truly found.

AS YOU WANDER

1. Forever Young

"Young people, it's wonderful to be young! Enjoy every minute of it. Do everything you want to do; take it all in. But remember that you must give an account to God for everything you do. So refuse to worry, and keep your body healthy. But, remember that youth, with a whole life before you, is meaningless. Don't let the excitement of youth cause you to forget your Creator. Honor him in your youth before you grow old and say, "Life is not pleasant anymore."
-Ecclesiastes 11:9-12:1 (NLT)

What a wonder to be young!

Getting your license. The first day of school. Moving to a new place for the summer or semester. New friends. Road trips. Adventures. First loves. Second loves. Dances. All-nighters. Sunrises. Broken bones. Failures. Growing pains. Joy. Life.

Being young sometimes is like a rollercoaster ride that may take off before you're even strapped in! The excitement is in the ups and downs that take your breath away and the unknown destination that lies before you. Guess what? God designed it that way. He adores your youth and Ecclesiastes says he wants you to "enjoy every minute of it."

Don't buy into this made-up God wagging his finger at you, telling you all the do's-and-don'ts of life. God is actually the creator of youth. He's the friend on the front row of the roller coaster in a backwards ball cap, strapped in and along for the crazy ride with you!

Give your youth back to God. He desires your heart and honor now, wanting to open your eyes to the wonder of His astounding creation. Let him jump into the seat beside you and laugh with you through the drops, twists, and turns. Find comfort in knowing that he designed how the ride begins, ends and everything else in between.

Please. Remember God now, don't just recall Him later.

Journal or Doodle:

What picture do you typically have in your mind when you think of God? Does seeing him as the creator of youth and fun shift your view? Will you let God ride with you through life?

2. What's my Calling?

"There are different kinds of gifts, but the same Spirit distributes them. There are different kinds of service, but the same Lord. There are different kinds of working, but in all of them and in everyone it is the same God at work."
-1 Corinthians 12:4-6 (NIV)

If you've attended a Christian circle for any amount of time, you've probably heard this word "calling." It sounds so mystical and spiritual. Like it only belongs to missionaries and pastors. However, we all have a calling and it's actually not as complicated to discover as it seems. Want to know what your God-given calling is? Let's start with this one truth:

A "calling" isn't something you're mediocre at or that everyone gets a trophy for. It is as radically simple as the thing that brings you joy and discovering God's purpose for that unique passion.

Discovering who God has called you to be is to distinguish between what you think you're good at and what you actually are.

You are an awesome latte maker. You have the incredible ability to light up a room with your smile. You plan awesome parties. You are a student, teacher, giver, and life-bringer. When you take the time to focus on your joy, you become excellent at sharing it. And, that is what God has called you to do.

The "different" that 1 Corinthians 12:4-6 is talking about is the definition of "calling." What brings you joy isn't the group trophy but the individual award God gave you and only you.

To discover your calling, take a look at your trophy case. What gifts and talents has God given uniquely you? What have you earned through your hardships? What ability do you have that could help others? Set joy as your compass it will always point you towards your life's purpose.

Journal or Doodle:

Have you ever heard the word "calling" before? What did you think it meant? What does it mean to you now and what are some things you believe God has called you to do?

3. Around Your Age

"Good morning! You're beautiful with God's beauty, beautiful inside and out! God be with you."
- Luke 1:28 (MSG)

Did you know that Mary, the mother of Jesus, was around your age?

The Jewish tradition of that time was that girls were married around 12 or 13 years old. It's estimated by some scholars that Mary was probably between 13 and 14 when she gave birth to Jesus.

Can you imagine packing your bag for class one morning and an angel of God appearing to you? What would it be like hear those words spoken to you just like they were shared with Mary in Luke 1:28? "You are highly favored!" "You're beautiful with God's beauty!" "The Lord is with you!"

While there will never be another young woman called to bring Jesus into the world, there is an all-call for every young woman to be Jesus to the world around her.

It's estimated that Mary mothered Jesus, David was anointed to be king and killed Goliath (1 Samuel 16-17), and Esther became a queen and saved her people (Esther 2) all during their teen to young adult years.

You see, back in the day the word "teenager" and "college-age" didn't exist. They are classifications our modern society has made up, making it seem like these are the years to put your faith on pause and live it up for yourself. However, God has great things planned for your life right now. So, don't let your youth hold you back from reaching for your God-given goals and dreams.

God clearly has used young adults to change the course of history in the past and will not stop presently. You are the key to revival in your nation, movers and shakers for the Gospel in our government, and the carriers of Jesus' love to the world.

Journal or Doodle:

Your legacy and impact start now. What great things will you allow God call you to today? How can you pursue a God-given dream in your future?

4. How Far Is Too Far?

"Flee from sexual immorality. All other sins a person commits are outside the body, but whoever sins sexually, sins against their own body. Do you not know that your bodies are temples of the Holy Spirit, who is in you, whom you have received from God? You are not your own."
-1 Corinthians 6:18-20 (NIV)

How far is too far? That's the question we're asking when it comes to relationships. It may seem like there are some gray areas about physical intimacy and sex. But, we can the truth by talking about warning signs.

At every mountaintop, you'll find warning signs. "Warning. Do not get close to edge. Death or injury may occur." "Warning. Cliff ahead. Do not hike off path." Warning ... warning ... warning.

What if I'm curious to see what's below? I disregard the warning. I inch carefully past the sign and closer to the edge. Out of nowhere, a huge gust of wind picks up. Because I'm shaky and unstable, I lose my balance and go over the cliff.

When we're wondering, "How far is too far?" What we're really asking is, "I see the warning signs. I know the risk. But I'm curious. How close to the edge can I really get without falling off?"

Here's your answer: 1 Corinthians 6:18-19 says, "Flee." Back up. Follow the path God has laid out for you. This isn't to keep you from exploring or enjoying your dating journey; it's to keep you from getting hurt.

It's to save your heart and body from having to repair before you can walk into the relationships God has for you.

When we're dating, and disregard God's warnings, we enter unstable, uncharted territory. If we cross that boundary line, all it takes is one push from that hot guy and we're over the line.

So, let's stop asking, "How far is too far?" It's a bad question steeped with uncertainty. Instead, obey the warning signs. Redirect your thoughts and ask, "How can I honor God and this boy I'm dating so that we both come out of this journey whole and happy?"

Journal or Doodle:

What has your dating journey been like so far? What safety steps do you need to put into place so that you can enjoy the adventure without crossing boundaries you'll regret? Draw a warning sign and write in it the section of 1 Corinthians 6:18-20 that stands out the most to you.

5. Shake Well

"And when they had prayed, the place where they had gathered together was shaken, and they were all filled with the Holy Spirit and began to speak the word of God with boldness."
-Acts 4:31 (ESV)

My favorite part of elementary school was strawberry milk.

I had enjoyed chocolate milk during my first lunch as a student in kindergarten. So, you can imagine my surprise when the lunch lady asked me, "Would you like chocolate or strawberry milk?" What! Strawberry milk is a thing? "Strawberry please!"

Thus, my love for strawberry milk began. I'd sit down at lunch every day, grab my little pink milk carton and follow the instructions on the tab. "Shake well."

One time, I made a huge mistake. I forgot to shake the milk carton. I opened it up to take a sip and tasted nothing but normal milk. It was disgusting.

If you're wondering what it means to have the Holy Spirit inside of your heart, it's like having strawberry syrup in milk. The moment we accept Jesus as our Savior, he pours into us the Holy Spirit. He's there, at the core of us, but to get the full effect we have to allow our lives to be stirred up for Jesus and poured out in love.

Some people walk through their lives every day with a bland and boring faith. They don't pray risky prayers, like asking God to specifically heal someone or fix something. They believe in miracles for others but never think they'll actually receive one for themselves. They are a Christian but look just like every other carton on the shelf.

We don't have to be regular. We can be revolutionaries! We can allow our hearts to be broken for what hurts the heart of God. We can let passion and love stir us up and send us out into the world. We can allow faith to disperse throughout our lives when any problem or obstacle shakes us up.

To access the Holy Spirit, look at the label that God has put on your life and follow the instructions, "Shake well."

Journal and Doodle:

Would you describe your faith: bland or shaken up? How can you allow the Holy Spirit to move in and through your life?

6. Warning Signs

"Your enemy the devil prowls around like a roaring
lion looking for someone to devour."
- 1 Peter 5:8 (NIV)

Freshly fallen snow created a soft blanket for the hard
mountain earth as we began our hike around the
valley in between the Maroon Bells.

The Bells are two mountains that have been given the
charming nickname "The Deathly Bells" and now I
know why.

We were heading around the lake when the couple
who had been hiking in front of us began to bolt like
lightening back down the path. Out of the forest
emerged a charging moose, head bowed with the
intention of piercing anything in his way with his
broad antlers. It was mating season, we were in his
territory, and he let us know.

"WARNING: MOOSE IN THE AREA" read the sign back
at the trail head followed by steps of action on what to
do if you encounter one. My thoughts weren't of
danger, but more or less that we might get to observe
a friendly moose from a safe distance. However, we
had quite the opposite experience of an adrenaline
rush while running for our lives from full fledge
moose attack. I should have taken the sign more
seriously...

The Bible also gives warnings we tend to overlook
such as, "WARNING: YOUR ENEMY THE DEVIL
PROWLS AROUND LIKE A ROARING LION."

There is wisdom in warnings, especially ones listed in the Bible. They are not signs posted in the ground that we pass on our way out the front door in the morning. But, we must stay keenly aware of our surroundings and understand that the problems we're running from may be related to the fact that there is a hunt for our souls.

So, what do we do about this warning about the "roaring lion?" How can we defend ourselves from the devil? The Bible is our great instruction manual and today, I challenge you to read the signs and know that the direction you can always run to for safety is towards Jesus.

Journal or Doodle:

Has the Bible ever told you not do to something and you did it anyway? How did that go? What does it look like for you to take God's warning signs seriously and protect yourself from any of the enemy's attacks?

7. A Dangerous Creature

"I have hidden your word in my heart that I might not sin against you."
-Psalm 119:11 (NIV)

"What book are you reading?"

My great grandmother, Maw-Maw, would lean over a bowl of cantaloupe, look at me through wide lens glasses and ask me this question every time I saw her. When I'd answer something that sufficed, she'd give me some quarters. Those pieces of fruit, change, and conversation were some of my sweetest, richest childhood memories.

This was a timeless question that would beg the rest of my life. I quickly learned from Maw-Maw that the ability to read for a woman is unique and powerful, a luxury in some places. It's a gift women in our country and across the world have not always had. Some still don't have.

Look— read your books. I don't know if anyone has ever told you that it's cute to play dumb but the reality is that it's stunning to be educated and well read. What a gift to retain the classics, fairy tales, nonfiction and fiction. We can be filled with the knowledge of history and futuristic ideas. We're to understand what our Bible *really* says.

Picking up a book is a way to lift your mind to places it cannot go on its own. So, hold pages instead of phones once in a while. Sit on your front porch with hot tea and a Bible and be transported to Jesus' world. Be wrapped up in another story because it will help you understand and write your own.

One of my favorite quotes from Lisa Kleypas says this, *"A well-read woman is a dangerous creature."* Why? Because, she is confident and courageous, truly knowing herself, God's Word, and worlds that exist beyond her.

Journal or Doodle:

What is your favorite book you've ever read? What is your favorite book of the Bible? How do you think retaining those has impacted your life? What book could you pick up right now?

8. Already Been Chewed

"Taste and see that the LORD is good; blessed is the one who takes refuge in him."
-Psalm 34:8 (NIV)

"Do you want some ABC gum?"

As a kid, when someone asked you this question, you quickly learned to say, *"NO!" Why?*

ABC wasn't a cute brand name; it stood for "Already Been Chewed." If you said "yes," your friend would spit out a saliva covered, flavorless wad into your open hand. It was hilarious as a ten-year-old... and disgusting.

The thing is, a lot of us are probably not willing to accept any ABC gum, but we're totally ok with an ABC faith.

We listen to our pastors and podcasts. We are reading Christian books every now and again. These things are great! However, if these are our only source of investment into our faith, we're basically just re-digesting someone else's thoughts. We're creating a relationship with Jesus based off someone else's relationship.

"Oh taste and see that the Lord is good" for yourself. Come to His table, sit down, and get to know Jesus one-on-one. Open your Bible and ask Him to teach you something. Pray directly to Him and talk about your thoughts and feelings.

It's great to hear about the character of Christ, but it's best to know Him for yourself.

Journal or Doodle:

If you've ever fallen for the ABC gum trick or played it on someone else, how gross was it? If you've had an ABC faith, what can you do today to get to know Jesus personally? If you're looking for somewhere to start reading in your Bible, try reading a chapter from Psalm or Proverbs every day for a week.

9. Fight Your Battle

"Then Saul dressed David in his own tunic. He put a coat of armor on him and a bronze helmet on his head. David fastened on his sword over the tunic and tried walking around, because he was not used to them. "I cannot go in these," he said to Saul, "because I am not used to them." So he took them off."
- 1 Samuel 17:38-39 (NIV)

You cannot win your battle in someone else's armor.

Have you heard the story of David and Goliath? David is a scrawny teenager that decides to slay a giant in a war he wasn't old enough to fight in. The king at the time, Saul, tries to protect David by at least giving him some armor to wear.

What happens? I imagine he straps on all that heavy gear and it weighs his awkward teenage body down. The metal clangs around, his feet shuffle under the weight, and he can't quite see out of the helmet on his head. So what does he do? He takes it off.

We have so much to learn from this moment! How often do we put on other people's armor and pray it does the trick for us? We ride the coattails of someone else's faith instead of developing our own relationship with Jesus. We crumble under the weight of heavy labels society has placed upon our shoulders instead of living out the truth of who God says we are. We hope what our pastor says is enough to get us through instead of developing any Bible study tools of our own.

Just like David, we're walking into the battlefields of our lives weighted down by what doesn't actually work for us. So, what should we do? Take it off! Any kind of protection from evil that may come your way is great. However, it may not all work for you and you have to get involved enough in your fight to find out.

Does Bible study work better for you in the morning, at night, or during your class break? When you've faced hardship before in your past, what tools did God give you to overcome and how can you use those today? How can you let go of the unnecessary weight of performance you put on yourself?

David defeated Goliath with just a slingshot and some stones. What about you, Warrior? What has God placed in your hand?

Journal or Doodle:

Take a moment to sift through the questions above. Answer all that seem to apply to you. Doodle a picture of what your God-given armor looks like.

10. What Will You Choose?

"Not only so, but we also glory in our sufferings, because we know that suffering produces perseverance; perseverance, character; and character, hope."
-Romans 5:3-4 (NIV)

We make millions of choices in a day. There's the little stuff like what to wear, eat, and post on our social media account about what we're wearing and eating. But then there's also the big stuff like what to write for our test, who to date and what we believe in.

I remember praying for peace over and over and being mad that God never gave it to me. "Hello God, there is a Bible passage that says you'll give me a peace beyond understanding (Philippians 4:7)!!" Here's what I've realized:

When you pray for things that are a development of character (like a greater faith, more joy, wisdom, etc.) God doesn't always just dump it into your lap. He often gives you a choice.

We get to choose peace over worry. Faith over fear. To speak life or death. To hold a grudge or extend grace. To repeat that bad behavior or pick a better path. God doesn't necessarily want to give us handouts because he wants these character traits to become learned behavior, a choice that sinks down deep into our soul and marks the rest of our decisions for life.

We have freedom and are in charge of our lives. So, let's opt to live our best one and make our best decisions. It's a choice we'll never regret.

Journal or Doodle:

What is the hardest or most complicated choice you have to make right now? How can you let God's Word and spiritual direction influence your decision? Write both sides of your decision across from each other and draw a big greater than or less than symbol (> or <) with the open end facing the way you know God wants you to choose.

There's a billion little choices to love every day.

AS YOU WANDER

11. Love from a Drunk Friend

"Love is patient, love is kind. It does not envy, it does not boast, it is not proud. It does not dishonor others, it is not self-seeking, it is not easily angered, it keeps no record of wrongs. Love does not delight in evil but rejoices with the truth. It always protects, always trusts, always hopes, always perseveres."
-1 Corinthians 13:4-7 (NIV)

I don't have a big solution for all the social media bullying, school shootings, or increasing depression and suicide rates among teens and young adults. However, I did have a friend that got really drunk once.

She stumbled into my home after a college party and headed straight for the bathroom where she proceeded to hurl uncontrollably. I went in, held back her hair and rubbed her shoulders. I couldn't make the puking stop but I could offer a little comfort in the process.

I could've yelled at my friend when she came in the door because I didn't want her to be drunk. I could have scolded her for all the things she did wrong. I could have explained to her my opinions. But, I saw the more important thing: she was sick and needed help.

Your generation is going through a lot. It's digested so much pain. It's had to change and develop under a social media microscope. You could yell at each other, tell someone all the ways they're wrong, or distance yourself from another race or religion because unity is hard and uncomfortable. Or, you can see the more important thing, that your peers are hurting and need the love of Jesus.

Maybe it's time that Christian young women simply step up to help their generation. To not beat up the bullies, but show up for the oppressed and marginalized. To speak from the Word and not their wounds. To offer some comfort while people are trying to get rid of the toxic things in their lives.

Journal or Doodle:

Take some time to identify areas you believe lack the love of Jesus in your generation. In the midst of blame and condemnation, how can you step into those places and offer comfort and care instead?

12. The Battle Is Not Yours

"This is what the LORD says to you: 'Do not be afraid or discouraged because of this vast army. For the battle is not yours, but God's.
-2 Chronicles 20:15 (NIV)

"Miss Independent." When my parents were informed I was getting an award in preschool, they probably were not expecting that one.

From my earliest years, I wanted to figure out everything by myself. How to tie my shoes, kick a soccer ball, and navigate the awkwardness of school, boys, and friends. I didn't need anyone because, look at me, I'm "Miss Independent."

I wore that badge proudly until one day at soccer camp. In the middle of running down the field, my whole world went black. I was immediately sent home where I was forced to go to the doctor. I HATE the doctor's office. Anybody else? The doctor told me I had dropped weight and was concerned. Just like that, my secret eating disorder was revealed and sports were taken away from me. To get on the field again, I had to gain the weight back.

In search for healing, (and because I now had nothing else to do) I sat in my room, played my guitar, and learned worship songs for hours. It was in that place that I wrote my first song and traded in my "Miss Independent" title for a life fully reliant on God.

At the time, my mom printed out 2 Chronicles 20:15 and put it on my mirror. This is the truth God spoke to

me then that He is still proclaiming over all of us who
have deep, internal battles. When the fight is too great
for us, we don't have to muster up the strength to
overcome it, we just have to stand still and let God
fight for us. We get to watch as he takes our
brokenness and makes it beautiful.

God will take the darkest points in our lives and
transform us to become the greatest lights in the
world. When we allow Him to fight for us, our wounds
become our worship, religion converts into an
intimate relationship with Jesus, and battlegrounds
become breeding grounds for our greatest blessings.

Journal or Doodle:

Have you ever felt like "Miss Independent"? What do
you need to do to take off that title and depend on
God? Take a moment to write or pray about a battle
you need God to fight for you. Note any blessings you
are discovering in the battle.

13. Choosing Your Spouse

"Be completely humble and gentle; be patient, bearing with one another in love. Make every effort to keep the unity of the Spirit through the bond of peace."
-Ephesians 4:2-3 (NIV)

"Besides deciding to follow Jesus, choosing your spouse will be the most important choice you'll ever make."

While I believe Christian culture means well, this phrase implies your entire life is riding on this choosing a spouse thing. I mean, it's up there with Jesus!

Here's what I think well-meaning Christians are really trying to say to those desiring marriage one day. Whoever you choose as your spouse is really important. They're going to be connected to you for life. However, besides deciding to follow Jesus, choosing your spouse isn't the most important decision you'll ever make and you don't need that pressure right now. Why?

1. You don't have a one and only soul mate. The pressure is off. They don't exist. You're actually looking for a teammate. Stop looking for the perfect person to date and find someone who will be unified with you in your vision for the future and compliment your love for life in the present (Ephesians 4:2-3).

2. Whoever you choose to marry isn't as important as how you choose to live during your dating life and marriage. It's not about finding

Prince Charming. You're really looking for someone who will authentically pursue the commitment you're making between each other and before God (Ephesians 5:25).

There isn't one weighty, future marriage decision. There are a billion little choices to love every day. They all start way before you walk down the aisle, at the moment you decide to walk with Christ. Choose this day to answer him when he asks if you'll receive his love with "I do." Live your life with God presently and allow him to direct you into the right relationships in the future.

Journal or Doodle:

Do you ever daydream about your wedding day? How can you turn that day and those desires over to God? By the way Jesus loves you, what standards does He set for the way you should be loved and treated in a relationship?

14. Not a "No"

"Ask and it will be given to you; seek and you will find; knock and the door will be opened to you."
-Matthew 7:7 (NIV)

A "no" from man isn't necessarily a "no" from God.

Michael Jordan was cut from his high school basketball team, someone told Thomas Edison he wasn't smart enough, Abraham and Sarah thought they'd never have children. The list goes on.

It's so easy to believe that when people slam the door in our face it's also a rejection from God. We go from chasing our dreams to rerouting our life the moment we hear, "You didn't make the cut."

Perseverance with our passions was greatly defined by author and speaker Mike Foster when he stated, *"When life shuts a door... open it again. It's a door. That's how they work."*

If our goals have received affirmation from friends and mentors and align with God's purpose, then a shut door isn't a "no" from God. It's more like a "not right now." It could be, "Keep working at it and push a little harder next time." Or, "I have something so much better in mind."

God has great plans for you. Let any rejection you've faced build resilience for your God-given hopes and dreams. Every "no" is a "yes" to something else so keep knocking and asking because one day the door will open.

Journal or Doodle:

What doors have shut in your face that made you want
to drop your dreams? Take a moment to rediscover
that passion. Brainstorm what doors you can open to
pursue it.

15. What God Wants

"Then the man said, "Let me go, for it is daybreak." But Jacob replied, "I will not let you go unless you bless me." The man asked him, "What is your name?" "Jacob," he answered. Then the man said, "Your name will no longer be Jacob, but Israel, because you have struggled with God and with humans and have overcome.""
- Genesis 32:26-28 (NIV)

God wants fighters.

When I read in the Bible about Jacob wrestling with God, Moses changing his mind, and people begging him to make good on his promises, I get a little uncomfortable. He is God after all. Can we really fight back, sway his decisions, and move his hands?

The crazy answer is yes. God wants us to participate in a relationship with him, not just follow the rules of religion.

When we wrestle with him through life's battles that means we are ridiculously close. When we can petition God, we know his true character as a Redeemer, Savior, Healer, and Good Father. When we can remind him of his promises like a child begging their parents, "But Mommy... but Daddy... you said," we've retained His Word, committed it to memory, and have enough faith to believe what he has said will come to pass.

I love this quote by Todd LaBerge: *"The greatest tragedy in humanity is when we do not wrestle with*

God, when we become so apathetic that we are but a limp rag doll in the hands of a mighty lover who wishes that we fight back, that we embrace him and choose to find truth. Christ will seek the ends of the earth for the one lost sheep that has gone astray. He will fight the darkness to find His beloved, but when He holds us in His arms and we do not show any sign of life, then it is the heart of a King that is broken and all creation will moan in the loss of another soul that was meant to dance in the courts of heaven."

LaBerge calls God a "mighty lover" because he absolutely is strong enough to handle our arguments and petitions and hold the weight we carry. He's willing to wrestle and chase us. So push back, plead, and remind him. However, don't become a "limp rag doll" in a world where you were born an action figure.

Journal or Doodle:

Is there an area in your life that you wish you could fight with God about, to let it all out and tell him how you really feel? Try it. Come back to this space and record any response you receive from him.

16. Until It's Good

"You intended to harm me, but God intended it all for
good. He brought me to this position so I could save
the lives of many people."
-Genesis 50:20 (NLT)

"It's not over until it's good."

How could he say such a thing? That car accident had
taken the lives of his toddler and newborn child. Our
community was devastated by this tragedy and, yet, in
the midst of it, the family it affected discovered a hard
truth that not many of us easily accept: All the time,
God is good.

You see, our lives change but God doesn't. Every time
we suffer, we're forced into making a decision
between allowing God to define our circumstances or
letting our situations change how we define God.

No one knew this quite like Joseph in Genesis 50:20.
Here's the quick recap of his life of suffering. When he
was your age, his brothers were so jealous of him they
sold him into slavery. As a slave, he was taken to help
an assistant to the Pharaoh in Egypt, Potiphar, whose
wife had Joseph thrown in jail. He was imprisoned for
years until Pharaoh summoned him to interpret his
dreams. This leads to the full circle story of Joseph,
because of his devotion to God, being elevated from a
prisoner to the ruler of the land in Egypt.

Plot twist! There was a great famine and one day his
brothers showed up to ask the ruler of the land in
Egypt (aka Joseph) for grain and didn't recognize him.

I'm paraphrasing here but, after a few meetings Joseph says, *"Surprise! It's me, your brother. See all the bad things you tried to do to me. Now look at all the great things God has done for me!"*

When we allow God to define our circumstances, he redefines our trials into triumphs. Our loss can become gain. Our prison transforms into a position of power. Our wound becomes our worship.

Like Joseph, you have been strategically positioned so that you too can "save the lives of many people." Whether in pain or in progress, remember that life change does not mean God's character or love for you has shifted. All the time, God is good. So, "It's not over until it's good."

Journal or Doodle:

When you're suffering, are you allowing God to define your circumstances or letting your situations change how you define God? If God is always good, what do you think that means will be the end result of your worst problem?

17. We Will Suffer

"I have told you these things, so that in me you may have peace. In this world you will have trouble. But take heart! I have overcome the world."
-John 16:33 (NIV)

Not might. Not maybe. Jesus promised us that we WILL have suffering.

This isn't a popular conversation topic because we want to believe that being a Christian will mean our life is easy. God is on our side so everything will be perfect now. Our prayers are heard so, poof! Amazing things are going to happen for us.

Here's the truth because I think you can handle it: Bad things happen to good people with great faith because we live in a broken world. That moment sin entered in made it impossible for all of us to escape hurt and pain. So, despite our prayers, our parents still divorce. Our future plans get ruined. Our heart gets broken. Things can get pretty ugly.

We have Jesus, not a genie, and following Him doesn't always lead us down the easiest path. Throughout the Bible we encounter people just like us who had some really hard times. They prayed and didn't hear answers right away. They messed up big time and had to face the consequences.

What they learned and what John 16:33 is telling us is that being a Christian doesn't make our life easy, it makes us come alive in the hardest of times. Despite suffering, we find peace because we know the Jesus who is well acquainted with pain, even to the point of death. While we may be in a bad place, God knows exactly where we are and will meet us there with his comfort and grace.

Both hurt and hope are guaranteed to us. The biggest difference that allows us to "take heart" is that hardship is temporary, God's love and our place with Him in heaven is eternal. Our life is not defined by our pain but our promise that, in Christ, we are overcomers!

Journal or Doodle:

What has caused your heart to hurt the most lately? What does it mean to you that Jesus completely sympathizes and feels what you feel? Will you allow God to meet you in your pain, suffer with you, and provide the hope and peace you need to bring you through?

18. Surrounded

"Then Elisha prayed, "O LORD, open his eyes and let him see!" The LORD opened the young man's eyes, and when he looked up, he saw that the hillside around Elisha was filled with horses and chariots of fire."
- 2 Kings 6:17 (NLT)

When it rains it pours, doesn't it?

It's not like we ever have just one little problem. It typically seems like everything goes wrong at once. We have that big test coming up, we can't get along with our parents and our best friend is really struggling. Our plans for the future got ruined, our heart was broken, and we feel so guilty about that choice we made on Friday night.

How does it feel when everything is going wrong? Like we're surrounded. The odds are against us and there is no way we will ever win this fight. If God is so good, where is he now?

If you've ever felt like this, you're not alone. A servant in 2 Kings 6:17 felt exactly the same way. He was with his master, a prophet named Elisha, when they found themselves surrounded by a great army. Just like us, he was overwhelmed and afraid.

However, the unimaginable happened. Elisha saw something that his servant didn't and prayed that his eyes would be opened. The servant's worries fell away as he noticed he wasn't outnumbered by enemies, but surrounded by countless members of the angel armies!

There's a lyric in one of my favorite worship songs, "Fight My Battles" by Upperroom, that says, *"It may look like I'm surrounded but I'm surrounded by you."*

My prayer for you today is 2 Kings 6:17. If you are surrounded by bad situations, sin and shame, may your eyes be opened. Yes, there is an enemy, the devil, who is against you. However, you are never alone. God is always fighting for you and his angel armies are by your side. You are not a victim surrounded by evil; you are the victor saved by Love!

Journal or Doodle:

What hard situations or circumstances surround you right now? Take a moment and ask God to open your eyes to see how he is fighting for you. Now, how do you see him working on your behalf?

19. The Antonym for Anxiety

"Don't fret or worry. Instead of worrying, pray. Let petitions and praises shape your worries into prayers, letting God know your concerns."
-Philippians 4:6 (MSG)

Have you heard this devastating statistic? The National Institute of Mental Health reports that somewhere between 25-38% of teens in America have been diagnosed with an anxiety disorder. That means that one out of four of your friends has struggled to the point they've sought medical or professional help. This is an epidemic! A plague! S.O.S. AMERICA! Clearly we need some help.

The antonym for anxiety is peace. So, when we're caught in the throes of anxiety, what can we do to bring the peace of God unto the situation? Philippians 4:4-7 gives us several major clues but here are three:

1. Give thanks- When we remember all God has done for us in our past and throughout the Bible, we know he has a bright future for us. The miracles he's done before he can do again.

2. Pray- Anxiety can seem like the loudest voice in our head. Prayer tunes our heart into God's voice and allows His truth to be heard above the noise. Ask Him to put peace as a safeguard over our heart and mind so that nothing else may enter.

3. Petition- This is praying with a stance on an issue until something happens. When we don't receive deliverance, we can argue with God that what we're experiencing doesn't line up with His peace. Ask Him to not only remove the anxiety but to join us in it.

Action plan: When anxiety creeps up, see it as an opportunity to experience Jesus in a new way. Be still and tell God what you're anxious about. Ask him to show you any areas you're not trusting him with, and to make himself apparent in those places. Wait for his presence to fill you there and practice carrying that every day. Once the peace of God has settled over your heart and mind, nothing can take it away. Then, may you have the authority over anxiety for yourself and others!

Journal or Doodle:

What do you think makes your generation have such an intense fear or pessimism about the days to come? Take a few moments to find encouraging quotes or Bible verses you can use to encourage yourself and others when anxiety strikes.

20. Jesus-Help

"For our sake he made him to be sin who knew no sin, so that in him we might become the righteousness of God."
-2 Corinthians 5:21 (ESV)

The Bible isn't a self-help book; it's a Jesus-help book.

Every magazine cover is littered with articles featuring steps to improve something about yourself. Books line shelves about how positive self-talk will lead to a positive life or claim to know the secret ingredient to a happier you.

Here's the spoiler alert for them all - 'Better You' will still not be 'Best You'. 'Better You' will let you down, make you think you're not good enough, and have room for improvements. 'Better You' is still you- wonderfully imperfect, quirky, and mending from a few bumps and bruises.

God didn't give us the Bible so we could find all these ways to grow and improve ourselves. He offered us his Word so that we can discover the path to the one who makes us righteous and redeemed. It's a love story to us - not a finger wagging, sin slamming, and five steps to success self-help book. The Bible points us to Jesus who doesn't make us better. He actually gives us His best.

Righteousness means (you guessed it) made right. Totally free from guilt or sin. See the great exchange here? Through Jesus, we're trading sin for salvation. Hurt for healing. Fighting for freedom. Anxiety for peace. Mistakes for miracles. 'Better You' for Best Jesus.

The best version of us will evolve out of following God and opening our Bibles. Why? Because throughout its pages we get to learn from the One who doesn't expect perfection but shows us how perfectly he loves. He doesn't force us to follow steps to improvement; he gently leads us step-by-step, day-by-day, through his grace.

Self-help is good but, really, there's only so much we can do for ourselves. Jesus-help is way better because he has the entire universe to offer. When your 'better' isn't cutting it, try asking for his 'best' instead.

Journal or Doodle:

What do you need the most help with right now? How can you trade that in for something Jesus has to offer?

Real religion is
love in motion.

AS YOU WANDER

21. Not an Audience, an Army

"For even the Son of Man came not to be served but to serve others and to give his life as a ransom for many."
-Matthew 20:28 (NLT)

"The Church isn't an audience it's an army," boldly stated Pastor David Chadwick.

What he and Matthew 20:28 are saying here is that we were never just meant to sit in a pew, sing some songs, sit through an hour-long service, and then go about our merry way. We're not to consume but to contribute. We're not here to be served but to serve.

Have you ever heard anyone refer to the church as a "house" and the congregants as "the family of God?" This paints an accurate depiction of the Biblical meaning of "church" because each family member in a house has their own unique responsibilities and gifts. Someone cooks, someone cleans, and someone tells the funny jokes. Someone makes holidays extra special, and someone is the planner for all the events. Each person has a part to play.

The same goes for God's house. We've all been given unique gifts and abilities. There are pastors and leaders, party throwers, deacons and elders, gardeners, cookie bakers, people who play music, others who greet, nursery workers, and volunteers who care specifically for high school and college ministries. There are a million different roles to play that make God's house a home.

Just as Jesus came "not to be served but to serve," we should show up in his house to help others. Whatever you have to bring to the table, He can use. The world needs your unique gifts. It's ironic how much you gain by giving yourself away.

Journal or Doodle:

If you volunteer at your church or in a local ministry, what do you do? How has that impacted your life? If you don't currently serve anywhere, what could you do to give back in your local church or community?

22. Let's Go Find Some Darkness

"You are the light of the world..."
-Matthew 5:14 (NIV)

"Did you get a headlamp?"
"Yes..."
"And you still have it?"
"Last time I checked..."

After a little rummaging through our already horribly stuffed camping pack, I found the first lamp and clicked the on switch. No light. Shaking it around a bit, I tried again. Still nothing.

You need to know, I was so broke at this time I couldn't afford a new headlamp, or even really the batteries required to make it work again. So, you can imagine my distress as I walked out into my poorly lit studio apartment and tried again. Hallelujah! A little beam of light shot out across the carpet floor.

What was the difference? Silly me, the lamp had actually been working the whole time! I was trying to see the light in a place that was already brightly lit.

This leads us to our real question: If we are the light of the world, why are we carrying it only into bright spots? Why are we willing to shine for Jesus in our churches and around specific friends but not in the classroom or work place where they can really be seen? Why are we not on mission in the mundane?

You see, it's so important that you don't keep your light hidden because we live in a dark world. Depression and anxiety are on the rise. Teen suicide rates continue to increase. Across college campuses, despite being surrounded by thousands of people, students report still feeling lonely. In order to find Jesus, the community you're in right now desperately needs the hope, joy and direction you have to offer.

You ARE the light of the world. So grab all you have to give and let's go find some darkness!

Journal or Doodle:

Where do you typically hang out and whom do you spend most of your time with? Would you describe it or them as dark or light? What is a dark place or person you could brighten up with God's love and your light?

23. Organized Chaos

"Create in me a clean heart, O God; and renew a right spirit within me."
-Psalm 51:10 (ESV)

I would've liked to call my dorm room organized chaos.

Most of my clothes didn't find their way to the hanger, socks were never paired together, and the only category that existed for my dresser drawers was "anything that doesn't belong in a closet." Where you might have been lost in the jungles of my dorm room, I felt at home. Despite the clutter, I knew where everything was. I was so content in the chaos because I created it.

Our souls are often a lot like my old room. We let the chaos build up because it's still functional. It may not be organized, but we know where our prayer life is, our desires lie, and what drawers our gifts and talents are stashed. We're content in the crazy because we created it. But organized chaos doesn't create a clean heart.

What about when we can't find what God is asking us to give him? The more junk we let gather in the corners of our lives, the harder it is for us to be thankful for what we have because we can't see it. Sometimes we may even forget that we possess these things and start complaining to God that we need what he has already given to us.

May we be good stewards of our soul and keep it clean. Maybe there are some cobwebs we need to sweep up, trash we need to take out, or some old life stories we need to reread that have been stored away in a drawer of our heart for too long.

Remember what God has done for you and take inventory of what you have been given. By this, thankfulness for what you have can give way to peace beyond circumstances.

Journal or Doodle:

How would you describe the state of your soul: Clean, messy, or organized chaos? Take some time to do inventory of your heart right now. What hidden hurts exist? What blessings have you forgotten? Bring all of this to God in prayer.

24. What Do I Do with My Future?

"Praise be to the God and Father of our Lord Jesus Christ, the Father of compassion and the God of all comfort, who comforts us in all our troubles, so that we can comfort those in any trouble with the comfort we ourselves receive from God. For just as we share abundantly in the sufferings of Christ, so also our comfort abounds through Christ."
-2 Corinthians 1:3-5 (NIV)

We all have this one very big question: What can I do with my future?

I remember darting up to the leader at a youth retreat to ask him this question, thinking a pastor for sure had all the answers.

Unexpectedly, he flipped the question on me in a way I'll never forget. "Well, what makes you cry?" I thought for a while and listed off some things. "Those things," he said, "THAT is how you'll change the world."

If you want to know what you're truly passionate about, do the hard and holy work of finding the place where you've been wounded. That is where hope is born, a desire for someone else to overcome the issue, and belief that love can heal. It all comes from your point of pain and this inspires almost all of your interactions and pursuits.

There's an old adage that says, "One man's trash is another man's treasure." It's true! Your hurt doesn't make you a throw away; it makes a healing balm to someone experiencing the same pain.

For example, my friend was sexually abused as a kid and now she helps women out of sex trafficking. Walking through an eating disorder in high school has inspired me to want to make sure that all women find mental and spiritual health. My sister struggled finding her own unique beauty and now she's a hair stylist and make up artist, unveiling authentic beauty in every woman she touches. What about you? How can you turn your hurt to healing and convert pain to passion?

That's the real question. Because, the bottom line is that no one can truly know what your future holds. However, you can certainly focus on what God has brought you to and through today. You can take some time to pinpoint the cause of your past pain and use it to get out and heal a broken world in the future.

Journal or Doodle:

What makes you cry? How can you turn your pain into a passion to pursue in the future? What does it look like for you to allow God to use your brokenness to heal others?

25. An 18-Wheeler Promise

"When Jesus spoke again to the people, he said, "I am the light of the world. Whoever follows me will never walk in darkness, but will have the light of life."
-John 8:12 (NIV)

We were asleep in our tent when the walls came crashing in. The thin rods that held the frame started nailing me in the face and whipping my body. What was going on!?

I unzipped the little window beside my head to look out but was blasted with sand.

The wind had picked up in the night, creating a tunnel between the giant rock faces that lined our campsite and was hurling dust through the air.

Deciding we couldn't stay and sleep because of the sand storm, we packed up camp at record speed and jumped in the car. We decided to head off to our next destination, Las Vegas, Nevada.

What we didn't know is that this windstorm had stretched across almost the entire western part of the country, causing snowstorms in places, especially the whole stretch between Utah and Nevada. So, we spent what seemed a thousand hours driving through blizzards in the dark.

We probably would have fallen straight off a cliff or ended up stranded in the desert if it weren't for an 18-wheeler. It seemed to travel our exact route. Its huge tires plowed a path for us through the snowy terrain and its lights were a beacon pointing us on the road ahead. It saved us.

Life is like that. We get hit, blasted even, by unexpected and unwelcomed events. We become blinded by our circumstances. However, we have an 18-wheeler promise from Jesus that says, *"Whoever follows me will never walk in darkness, but will have the light of life."*

If you're wandering right now through a sand or snowstorm in your faith journey, keep moving. If you stop, you'll become stranded. You will have the hardest time restarting. So, ease on the gas and follow the path God has paved for you. You don't even have to be certain of where you're going. Just follow the light.

Journal or Doodle:

What is an unwelcomed or unexpected event that has blinded you lately? How can you keep focused on the path God is paving for you when the way seems hard?

26. More Like Martha

"But Martha was distracted by all the preparations
that had to be made. She came to him and asked,
"Lord, don't you care that my sister has left me to do
the work by myself? Tell her to help me!" "Martha,
Martha," the Lord answered, "You are worried and
upset about many things, but few things are needed -
or indeed only one. Mary has chosen what is better,
and it will not be taken away from her."
- Luke 10:40-42 (NIV)

What if you went over to your grandma's house for
Thanksgiving dinner and nothing was prepared?
When you asked her about the special meal, she just
replied (in a very southern accent because that's how
my Maw-Maw would have said it), "Lorrrddd, I was
just worshipping God."

Wouldn't you be shocked? Sad even. Like, God is great.
God is good. But, I want to thank him for our food.
Well, that's the situation Martha was in as stated in
Luke 10. She invited Jesus and all his disciples over to
her home for dinner. As a woman, she was expected
by her culture to serve the men. Just like we wouldn't
hate on grandma for cooking Thanksgiving dinner, we
shouldn't think Martha was a crazy woman for serving
Jesus. You'd serve him too.

Mary, however, is breaking all cultural rules. She's a
woman not fulfilling her societal or even family role
while her sister is trying to prepare a huge
dinner. Martha needs some help while Mary is chilling
at Jesus' feet. So, why was that the right thing to do?

When we're serving Jesus and using our gifts, we're not doing anything wrong. However, when our service overrides God's ability to serve us then we should probably sit down.

Jesus is not condemning Martha for working hard, he's caring for her because she's overworked. What he's saying to her is intended for us all. *"I'm all you need. I'm the bread of life, the very thing that is going to make all of us full. So, before you feed others, fill yourself."*

This passage isn't a free for all to not do anything but sit in God's presence. It's actually a call to allow God to pour into us so that we can overflow into others.

Journal or Doodle:

Are you serving others before you're allowing Jesus to serve you? If you feel depleted, what does it look like for you to sit at Jesus' feet to rest and reenergize?

27. Big Fears with Great Faith

"Have I not commanded you? Be strong and courageous. Do not be afraid; do not be discouraged, for the LORD your God will be with you wherever you go."
-Joshua 1:9 (NIV)

The areas God wants us to make an impact are precisely the sites Satan wants to attack. Satan wants to cripple the biggest moments in our lives with fear and anxiety.

So, how do we weed out the fear Satan is trying to sow into our lives and plant ourselves deeply into the faith we were meant for?

Let's take a look at Joshua 1:9 for some answers. Joshua was actually Moses' sidekick so to speak and, after Moses' death, God asked Joshua to take his leader's place. That's like telling Robin to be Batman, Piglet to be Pooh, or Chewbacca to be Han Solo. You better believe it was not only uncomfortable for Joshua, but probably very intimidating. He had some great shoes to fill plus a big commission to take the Promised Land and lead the Israelites into freedom (read the rest of the book of Joshua for the full story).

His initial response, just like you and me, must have been a little bit of fear, some doubt, and a wave of worry. We know this because God almost immediately says, "Be strong and courageous (v.9)."

We can take a stance of courage by noting where Satan is trying to erect walls of fear to keep us out of our Promised Land. We tear them down brick by brick as we reclaim our territory by replacing fear with faith. We're taking back our land and lives on these grounds:

God has called us up, even in our little living, into big positions. He's asked us to step out boldly in our gifting and be women who fearlessly fight for our friends, communities, and world. And we lead those around us into freedom.

Though walking out our faith is a bit scary, God feels what we feel. He sees our knees knock and hears our voices of doubt and discouragement. He instills in us the strength to overcome our biggest fears with great faith.

Journal or Doodle:

What area of your life do you think Satan is trying to cripple you with fear? How can you tear down the walls he's trying to build in your life with faith? For what or whom will you fight for?

28. Do It Again!

"I will proclaim your name to my brothers and sisters.
I will praise you among your assembled people."
-Psalm 22:22 (NLT)

Did you know that the word "testimony" at its root
means "do it again?"

A big part of my testimony is that underneath being a
Christian, student leader, three-sport athlete, an "A"
student, I hid a secret eating disorder through high
school.

Most people attribute that to a body image issue but,
for me, it was a control problem. I couldn't make
myself fit in, a guy I dated cheated on me, the rumors
and the bullying had crushed my spirit but I wanted to
appear strong. On top of it all there was the constant
pressure of "what are you going to do in the future?"

When life was spiraling, I wanted to make it stop so I
held onto what felt like the only thing I could control -
eating.

I look back on that girl who had wasted away on the
outside and realize it was a physical manifestation of
how I felt on the inside. I want to tell her about a
bright future, how good it was going to get in college,
and let her know that there's more security in Godly
surrender than personal control.

I can't go back to that girl but I can go to you and say,
"God, do it again!" I can tell you my story so that you
can change yours. When you have disordered

thinking, holy thinking can reorder it (2 Timothy 1:7). If you feel frail, God is stronger (2 Corinthians 12:7-10). Your praise is greater than your problems and chains are broken when we simply believe in our Jesus given right to freedom (Acts 12:6-7).

Pastor David Chadwick says, "Work from victory not for victory." In other words, whatever you're going through, work backward. See yourself as the whole, strong, beloved woman that God has called you to be. In the midst of the fight, realize that you've already won the victory. You're going to make it.

Journal or Doodle:

What's your testimony? Write it or draw it here. In giant letters at the end write, "GOD, DO IT AGAIN." Make that your prayer today and see if there's anyone who needs to hear your story so they can be inspired to rewrite theirs.

29. Mentors and Mentees

"Likewise, teach the older women to be reverent in the way they live, not to be slanderers or addicted to much wine, but to teach what is good. Then they can urge the younger women to love their husbands and children, to be self-controlled and pure, to be busy at home, to be kind, and to be subject to their husbands, so that no one will malign the word of God."
- Titus 2:3-5 (NIV)

Hands in the air. Sold out to the message. Freely worshipping.

Sitting there behind the sound booth at a middle school retreat one weekend, Titus 2: 3-5 came to my mind as I watched passionate kids be supported, prayed over, and cheered on by their older student leaders.

You see, there is a call for women to influence those older and younger than us. We're to be both mentors and mentees. This is how we grow in the Wander years, as high school and college-age girls reaching up and down to gather and give all we can.

If you're feeling stagnant in your faith, it's time to look around you. Ask someone older and younger than you to meet for coffee, offer them the opportunity to help you grow, and learn and teach all you can.

If you already have a mentor, I challenge you to leave her a note of encouragement that lets her in on how much she's teaching you. If you have a mentee or mentees, encourage them by sending them a text stating exactly where you're seeing them grow in their faith.

We are women of the Word, influencers of the generations, and champions of encouragement and growth. We can't do this without each other.

<u>Journal or Doodle:</u>

If you don't have a mentor or mentee, list three people you think you could reach out to. If you do, write their names below. Pray specifically over each name. What are some things you want to talk about in your next conversation with them? What do you want to learn from a mentor and what can you teach to a mentee?

30. Oh, That's Religion!

"Religion that God our Father accepts as pure and faultless is this: to look after orphans and widows in their distress and to keep oneself from being polluted by the world."
-James 1:27 (NIV)

Maybe you've been thinking religion is rules, church every single Sunday, and boring Bible study.

However, James tells us something much more exciting. The Biblical definition of religion is finding the forgotten, supporting the suffering, and being cultural rebels with a cause.

As an intern at Operation Christmas Child during college, I was in charge of getting the children's choirs on and off stage for one of the big events. A teacher and I struck up a conversation in the waiting room. We had trips to Africa in common and I was telling her about all the orphans that I had cared for and missed. She replied with one of the most eye-opening statements I've ever heard:

"There are orphans all around us here, too. They may not be on the streets abandoned. They're probably in schools and clubs and sports. They're in our churches. They even have two parents. The orphan epidemic in America is a result of having parents who have forgotten to love their kids well. Some are here in front of you right now."

As those kids stood on the stage and sang their hearts out, I saw them. For the first time, with their clean faces and normal every day clothes, I saw them. Those orphans I'm called to help aren't just in Africa; they were there in the room next to me.

You see, orphans and widows are right in front of us every day. They're our classmates who have parents that don't invest in them. They are people in our church with secret struggles. They are friends in mourning pretending to be rejoicing.

Real religion is love in motion so let's get busy living it out for our neighbor in need!

Journal or Doodle:

Before reading James 1:27, how would you have defined religion? How will you redefine and act on it now? Can you identify some hidden orphans or widows in your community? If so, take a moment to write out a prayer for them.

*Sometimes God shows
himself to us in the worst
interruptions of our
best-laid plans.*

AS YOU WANDER

31. The Religious Rebel

"Jesus answered, "I am the way and the truth and the life. No one comes to the Father except through me."
-John 14:6 (NIV)

Jesus was criticized by the Pharisees, the super pastors of Biblical times, for doing scandalous things like hanging out with sinners, standing up for people of different races and walks of life, and healing people on the Sabbath. Jesus was a religious rebel because he was setting the example he wants us to follow. He wants you to know that life isn't about following all the rules of religion but being in a relationship with God.

Author and speaker Rebecca Manley Pippert puts it this way, "It is a profound worry that the Son of God visited this planet and one of the chief complaints against him was that he was not religious enough."

We live in a world where performance is applauded. Success is defined by how busy we are, how much we can accomplish, and all we can earn. However, the ability to connect with Jesus is a free gift. Our salvation isn't something we can earn. You get full access to heaven, grace and love the moment you decide to walk with God.

You see, Christianity isn't about rule following but Jesus following. It's the totally accepting, freeing relationship with him that leads us to obedience, not the other way around.

If you've been struggling with the thought that you've

messed up too many times to be loved by God, remember that Jesus came to save us ALL: the saints and the sinners, the imperfect and the broken, the hopeful and the helpless. There is level ground at the foot of the cross so come as you are!

Journal or Doodle:

Do you identify with the Pharisees, feeling like you have to be perfect to be accepted by God? Or are you more of a religious rebel, breaking all the rules and believing you're too messed up to be loved? What do you think is the biggest difference between following all the Christian rules and actually being in a relationship with Jesus?

32. Instead of Ashes

"To all who mourn in Israel, he will give a crown of beauty for ashes."
-Isaiah 61:3 (NLT)

I left on this journey as ashes, burnt out from all the things that used to ignite a passion in my heart, and I was seeking fire again.

Really, burnout is an epidemic sweeping throughout our nation. Our need to be needed, tendency to compare ourselves to one another, and desire to contribute something grand to society causes us to build bonfires out of our lives without gathering any wood to keep the fire going.

Are you burnt out in areas that you used to have passion for? Do you find yourself going through the motions when you used to be excited to act? God desires for you to find your flame again. Here are three questions I have been asking myself that will hopefully help you too.

1. Who are you doing this for?
This answer is your log, what your fire is built upon, so be genuine. If your answer is the same as when God birthed it in your heart, keep going. But if it has changed from that moment, reorient your focus.

2. Why do you have a passion to do this?
This is your fire starter. What is the first thing that ever sparked your fire and is it still driving you forward? If it's not, write down a few memories from the start of your faith walk or life goals. Look back at

old pictures. Note how your passion has developed and is expanding but don't lose sight of the match that lit your first flame.

3. How are you fueling your fire?
In the same way you have to keep putting logs into a fire to keep it burning, you have to continually remember your answers to the first two questions. As time goes on, you'll need to add in different things and bigger logs. Ask God what those look like and who should come along to help you build your fire now.

God wants to replace the ashes of your desires with new dreams. Find and fuel your own flame so that you don't burn out chasing someone else's fire. And grow, so that you are a light in for dark world to see.

<u>Journal or Doodle:</u>

Take a moment to answer the three questions above. What did you discover? If you're experiencing burn out, what steps can you take to reignite the fire of your faith?

33. Healing the Rejection Wound

"He was despised and rejected— a man of sorrows, acquainted with deepest grief. We turned our backs on him and looked the other way. He was despised, and we did not care."
-Isaiah 53:3 (NLT)

We all have a rejection wound.

That guy broke up with us. One of our parents didn't invest in us. Our best friend hurt us so badly, we still can't really talk about it yet. We didn't get that job, into that college, or qualify for that group. We have ALL been there.

As a result, we think God will turn us away. Our resume won't be good enough for him. He won't accept what we have to offer. We simply don't make the cut when it comes to deserving Jesus' gift of salvation and a full life.

However, Jesus doesn't want to deepen our rejection wound but heal it. If we take a look at anyone that came to Jesus with an authentic heart in the Bible (we're talking prostitutes, murderers, and some serious sinners), he never turned them away.

Maybe it's because Jesus himself was so familiar with rejection (Isaiah 53:3). He was God and hated by the most religious people, a perfect man despised by the ones he came to serve and save, and the giver of life condemned to death on a cross. Trust me, Jesus gets it. He knows that rejection wound more than you'll ever know and, hallelujah, holds the power to heal it!

So, let's go to that verse that you may have been able to quote since you were three years old. John 3:16, "For God so loved the world that he gave his only son that..." who gets to receive eternal life? "WHOEVER." Not some. Not the favorites. Not the successful, perfect, pretty people. ANYONE who believes is chosen, accepted, and welcome in God's kingdom.

Rip off that rejection wound Band-Aid and let the hope of acceptance heal your broken heart!

Journal or Doodle:

Have you ever felt rejected? How does it make you feel to know that Jesus understands your pain and accepts you as you are?

34. Don't Waste Your Waiting

"Wait for the LORD; be strong, and let your heart take courage; wait for the LORD!
-Psalm 27:14 (ESV)

Isn't in incredibly tempting in times of waiting to idle? To wake up every morning and ask "Could this be the day I get all the answers? Will God actually come through for me?" We want to hide in a spiritual or situational bunker and refuse to emerge back out into life until God answers all of our prayers and gives us a clear answer.

However, God doesn't want us to waste our waiting. He doesn't want us to stop living just because we started longing. So what does he want us to do with all this anticipation?

John Piper answers this best in his book "Don't Waste Your Life." He says, *"God created me---and you---to live with a single, all-embracing, all-transforming passion---namely, a passion to glorify God by enjoying and displaying his supreme excellence in all the spheres of life... The wasted life is the life without a passion for the supremacy of God in all things for the joy of all peoples."*

Our waiting is wasted when, instead of participating in our passions, we settle for mundane moments of mulling over what could or will be. We miss out on the full preparation of becoming who God is calling us to be when we get so focused on waiting that we stop worshipping.

Instead of wasting our waiting, let's invest it. Spend less time looking for someone to date or marry and more into becoming the person you want to be when you get married. Prep for those college or job interviews and ask your Bible study group to pray specifically that you receive the answers you really want. Participate in God's will for your life, knocking relentlessly on those doors to your future until one of them opens.

Instead of allowing our waiting to paralyze us in the present, let's move forward into our future with hope.

<u>Journal or Doodle:</u>

What do you typically do when you're waiting on God to give you an answer? What can you do to keep from wasting seasons of expectation? Write down some things you're waiting on right now and a short prayer asking God how you can worship while you anticipate his answers.

35. Jesus Finally Came

"The beginning of the good news about Jesus the Messiah, the Son of God, as it is written in Isaiah the prophet..."
- Mark 1:1-2 (NIV)

Did you know that there is a 400-year gap between the Old and New Testament?

Four hundred whole years where God was seemingly silent while the world sat waiting on a Savior.

We think our prayers are taking a long time to get answered, right? Like, we prayed for that thing last week and we're already experiencing some anger and disbelief rising up for not receiving an answer already!

If we feel like that after a matter of days, can you imagine the anticipation after generations of people had lived and died before they ever heard an answer from God? Now, picture God not only answering those ancient prayers, but finding out he decided to come down from heaven and live as one of us!

Hallelujah! This is what the New Testament is all about. Jesus finally came so that we'd never have to be without Him again. From the cradle, to the cross, and onto the resurrection, he gave us free access to heaven and the ear of God forever.

Next time you're waiting on an answer to prayer, rest assured that God hears you, loves you, and has a plan for you. He already came as the promised Messiah and will come with his presence every day as the Holy Spirit. Wait patiently and eagerly, he always shows up and shows off in a greater way than we can ever expect.

Journal or Doodle:

What do you think it would have been like to live at a time when God seemed silent? How does that change your level of gratitude for the Holy Spirit being present among us today? If you're waiting on an answered prayer, how does this offer you fresh encouragement?

36. Rise Up Fighter

"Do not gloat over me, my enemy! Though I have fallen, I will rise. Though I sit in darkness, the LORD will be my light."
-Micah 7:8 (NIV)

"How long are you going to take this?" they asked. I was bawling after wrestling through another sleepless, anxious night. *"What do you mean?"* I blubbered. *"I mean you just keep letting your insomnia and anxiety hit you in the face. When are you going to hit back?"*

The fighter in me, who had seemed to vanish through the hardships of the past year, rose up suddenly. She started to reach down deep, down into her old self. Dust her off and put her back up on the shelf.

There was that old girl: fearless, brave, and courageously curious. How do I get back to her? What can we do to fight back against the fear and exhaustion that plagues our lives and robs us of ourselves?

I've never been a boxer but from what I understand, you not only have to hit back, you have to anticipate. Guard your face. Protect yourself and be one step ahead of the opposition.

Biblically here are 3 ways we can do this:

1. Pray with audacity, knocking relentlessly on God's door until he gives us what we need (Matthew 7:7).

2. Dismiss Satan's lies with God's truth (Philippians 4:8).
3. Fight from victory not for victory. Because we're on God's team, we know the end of the story— we get the K.O., the belt, the trophy, the heaven (John 16:33).

Rise up fighter. You've been hit hard. You have scars and bruises. But don't tap out. You're not only going to make it, you're going to beat it. Stay in the game. Just keep swinging.

Journal or Doodle:

Have you ever felt knocked down or out in life? Will you stand up today and protect yourself with God's Word? What's one step you can take to fight back against fear and become proactive in your faith?

37. Interruption or Opportunity?

"Don't bargain with God. Be direct. Ask for what you need."
-Matthew 7:7 (MSG)

"Class is cancelled for the day, check email for more information," read the front door of my classroom after I darted across campus in the snow for a mile to get there on time. *"Great,"* I thought, *"all that for nothing."*

On my begrudging walk home, a man walked by and placed a large pink pamphlet in my hand. Through a wide-mouthed grin he said, "Have a great day." I looked down and it was a whole listing of scriptures stating Jesus cares for me. That He died and resurrected for me.

Sometimes God shows himself to us in the worst interruptions of our best-laid plans. We often miss him because we mistake our opportunities as inconvenience.

Maybe we're supposed to grab coffee with a friend and she didn't show up. We may view this as an interruption as we drink our mocha with extra whipped cream and sulk on our phone in the corner booth. Or we can see this as an opportunity and buy the person's coffee behind us in line and say, "God bless you."

Possibly our best friend gets a boyfriend and stops talking to us. We can make it an interruption by becoming mad at her or we can transform it into an opportunity to pray for her. Instead of distancing ourselves, we can position ourselves to be there for support if the relationship ends.

That guy that broke up with you. That school you didn't get into. That dream that seems just out of reach. Matthew 7:7 says we can ask God for exactly what we need. So when things don't work out, we have to trust God is actually trying to give us something better than what we want. He's not inconveniencing us to be annoying; he's trying to create a better opportunity for us.

When our expectations fall through, God's can succeed. So when something doesn't go as we planned, ask him what he planned.

Journal or Doodle:

What is an inconvenience that may actually be an opportunity in your situation right now? How would your life change if you trusted that God's plans for you were better than anything you've planned for yourself?

38. From Commentators to Caregivers

"For I was hungry and you gave me something to eat, I was thirsty and you gave me something to drink, I was a stranger and you invited me in, I needed clothes and you clothed me, I was sick and you looked after me, I was in prison and you came to visit me... Truly I tell you, whatever you did for one of the least of these brothers and sisters of mine, you did for me.'"
-Matthew 25: 35-36; 40 (NIV)

Our social media driven society makes it easy to comment on other people's lives. We like pictures, share information and leave messages all day long.

While we can make a positive impact through social media, sometimes people need more. They want a shoulder to cry on, not a screen to look at. They've received a text but are desperate for real conversation.

Life is heavy, so let's put down our phones to help each other lighten the load. Let's move from being commentators to caregivers.

Caregivers commit. They personally invest in others. They show up to heal the sick, take responsibility for others and find the solution to someone's deepest need. They are unsung heroes because they're too busy living in the moment to capture it or snap it. They're out there creating a God-story, not just posting on one.

When we get to heaven, God isn't going to wonder how many social media subscribers we had. He is, however, going to ask what we did with our lives and how we helped others.

While being a social media commentator can be good, being a caregiver is what God values most in heaven and on earth.

Journal or Doodle:

What are some ways you can go from commentator to caregiver by serving in your community? What would it look like to act on one of your most encouraging social media posts or comments?

39. Dear Lord

"And the LORD said, "I will cause all my goodness to pass in front of you, and I will proclaim my name, the LORD, in your presence."
-Exodus 33:19 (NIV)

"Dear Lord..."

This is how I've started off my prayers for years. Possibly you too. And, whether in your Bible or in general conversation, you've probably heard God referred to as "Lord" before. Why? What does that really mean?

Well, for starters, let's talk about the big difference between having a Lord and being lorded over.

A Lord is a good, mighty leader. Another Hebrew word for this that could have been used in Biblical times is "Jehovah"- the most sacred word used for God. So sacred, in fact, that some wouldn't even say it aloud. It references dignity, the highest honor and majesty.

To be lorded over is to be dictated. To have someone boss or bully you around, making you feel unworthy of respect or honor. There are several examples of harsh dictators and tyrants from history books as I'm sure you can recall. Maybe even a terrible landlord from a college apartment or a really brutal teacher.

You see, God is our Lord, "Jehovah." He is holy, sacred, and the One you really want in charge. He's worthy of our honor because he's full of love, extending forgiveness and grace freely. Not lording over us by forcing us to love him back or earn our spot in heaven. He's a gentleman, letting us choose to follow him and telling us we don't have to be perfect to be perfectly loved.

Journal or Doodle:

Have you been viewing God as a harsh ruler over you or as your Lord and Savior? How can you trust and follow him as "Jehovah" today?

40. What Are You Set Apart For?

"For where two or three gather in my name, there am I with them."
-Matthew 18:20 (NIV)

"You do you, Boo-Boo." "Live your life." "Do what feels good."

These phrases are tossed around like confetti in our faces. We sit back and say, "Wow! Look at those beautiful, shiny, empowering words." We pick them up and try to throw them around in our own lives only to quickly realize that doing our own thing eventually makes us feel isolated and lost.

Modern culture has tried to make us believe that individuality is personality and it's not. Yes, we were made with some unique God-given character traits and talents. There is truly only one of us in the world. However, we were never meant to live our lives as individuals who standalone.

In fact, Satan is the god of isolation while Jesus is the God of community. Matthew 18:20 is proof that we experience God's presence most when we surround ourselves with other people. Community with people and God were designed not to take away from who we are but through support, accountability, and encouragement, help us become the best version of ourselves.

Here's the big truth: We were created by God, not to be set apart as individuals from him and his people, but to be set apart in our personalities and passion for him.

We only have to look at our fingerprint to know that we are all different. However, we are all unified by one great love from God. We each have a little part to play in his big story.

If you've been trying to operate as an individual, pray about how you can instead thrive in community. Your personality was meant not to set you apart from God but to set you apart for Him, drawing others to you that long to discover what it means to share in his love, radical acceptance, and community.

Journal or Doodle:

What do you think are the biggest differences in individuality and personality? What unique things do you think you have to offer to the community of God?

We can easily dismantle isolation by creating community right where we are.

AS YOU WANDER

41. Travel Light

"Travel light. Comb and toothbrush and no extra luggage... When you enter a home, greet the family, 'Peace.' If your greeting is received, then it's a good place to stay... When you enter a town and are received, eat what they set before you, heal anyone who is sick, and tell them, 'God's kingdom is right on your doorstep!'"
-Luke 10:4-14 (MSG)

I'm an expert at traveling light. Moving approximately every six months in college to new places and countries taught me how to open a suitcase, grab the necessities, and get out. Isn't there something exhilarating about being a vagabond? Going on a great trip, having only what you absolutely need. As if limited options give you more freedom. Less is more.

But, here's the thing; we travel light because God's kingdom is heavy. It's thick with relationships, exploration and seeing him in everything. It's in meals shared at long tables with strangers and friends alike. It's seeing the church in all her glory across states and nations and worlds. It's letting the Holy Spirit bind you, like family, to people and places you've never met. The kingdom is everywhere so you can go anywhere and find it.

No matter where you may go or who may come into your life, have an open door and heart. Unknowingly, you may have packed the blessing someone needs. You may be hosting angels (Hebrews 13:2). God's kingdom may be right over that "Welcome" mat on that distant doorstep.

Journal or Doodle:

Where are you right now and where do you dream about going? How have you discovered God's kingdom in unexpected places? What do you think it would look like in a foreign land?

42. Too Used to Be Usable

"The sacrifices of God are a broken spirit; a broken and contrite heart, O God, you will not despise."
-Psalm 51:17 (ESV)

I just read this awesome quote that says, "The last time I checked, broken crayons still color the same."

Do you remember as a kid coloring with crayons? I don't know about you, but I used to color aggressively. In an effort to make my lines perfect, I'd bare down around the edge of the figure I was shading. It never failed that at least one crayon either broke in half or was left without a tip.

Now I see my crayon box for what it was, a flimsy carton filled with chipped, peeled off wrappers and broken colors. However, as a kid, it was potential. A new image waiting to happen. A Lisa Frank inspired color explosion! There was so much beauty in all of those broken, worn down things.

Just like from Genesis to Revelation, God continued to see and use broken things in beautiful ways. His story and our story is that old things can be made new, the dead can be brought to life, there are miracles in the messes, and a light in the darkness.

Next time you think you're too used to be usable, remember all those masterpieces you created with cracked crayons as a kid. It doesn't matter if you're perfect to God, only that you're usable.

Journal or Doodle:

Have you ever felt like you're a mess and God can't forgive you? Or you've wandered too far away for him to still love you? What broken things do you need to put in God's hands and ask him to make something beautiful out of today? Take a few minutes to doodle a picture or word God is speaking to you about right now.

43. Happiness

"For it is written: Be holy because I am holy."
-1 Peter 1:16 (NIV)

God doesn't care as much about our happiness as He does our holiness.

My sister gave me a Willow Tree figurine named "Happiness." She's a chest open, head high, boldly forward-facing girl with blue birds perched on her shoulders.

I've taken "Happiness" with me everywhere I've traveled. As a result of being repackaged and shifted around a dozen times, she carries some bumps and bruises. Two of the bluebirds have chipped wings. A deep scratch adorns the front of her flowing white dress.

Despite her flaws, I still keep her front and center on my dresser. Here's why.

We are all God's daughters trying to fly with broken wings and heal with broken hearts. My angel of "Happiness" reminds me that real life doesn't look Pinterest perfect. It's going to break, mold and shape us. But that's okay because 1 Peter 1:16 tells us our destiny isn't to be happy; it's to be holy.

Happiness is an emotion, a thirst, which can never be quenched. That fleeting feeling will never fully satisfy. Holiness, however, fills us the moment we allow Jesus' redeeming love to overflow in our hearts. Holiness is God's light shining through our cracks. It stands on display to reveal the beautiful things Jesus has done in and through our brokenness.

May we all stand like "Happiness," flying with broken wings, boldly facing forward into a future full of hope, and choosing joy on our journey toward holiness and Jesus.

Journal and Doodle:

What life situations have broken your wings and left you with bumps and bruises? What beautiful things has God brought out of your brokenness? Find one thing you can set out on your dresser to remind you to choose joy and a life of holiness.

44. Selfie or the Savior

"But when you pray, go into your room and shut the door and pray to your Father who is in secret. And your Father who sees in secret will reward you."
- Matthew 6:6 (ESV)

Are you seeking the selfie or the Savior?

We log onto our Instagram and see the perfect set up. Bible, journal with beautifully scripted notes, cup of coffee, and a tiny succulent stashed in the corner. It's intimidating isn't it? To think every time you decide to be with God it should be like this. So often our most reverent moments are anything but Instagram worthy.

Real life is messy.

So, here's what happens when we're seeking selfie-worthy faith. We plan our lives to please others and stop allowing room for God's plans and affirmation. Whether on social media or in conversation, we only reveal our best side. We're so focused on "doing it for the gram (whatever "it" is)," we forget we're supposed to be doing it all for Jesus.

When we're seeking the Savior, we find secret, intimate places to meet with Him. We uncover the miracle in the mess. We stop scrolling through everyone's highlight reel long enough to get real.

That "like" button makes us believe we need others to validate our lives but the reality is that God has orchestrated great parts of our story that we don't even like. Those instances that impact us most might not belong on a gallery wall but they're really the moments we want to remember forever.

We have to want the Savior more than the selfie because salvation from Jesus is knowing we don't have to be picture perfect to be perfectly loved. Flip the lens on the selfie standard for your faith and see the Savior who is setting up the big picture of your life.

Journal or Doodle:

When you're tempted to make sure your faith looks picture perfect, how can you remind yourself that God may want to use a messy moment to impact your life? Does social media ever make you feel like you don't measure up to the standards of others? What does it mean to you that Jesus is the one setting up the big picture of your life?

45. Don't Miss the Messiah

"Teach these new disciples to obey all the commands I
have given you. And be sure of this: I am with you
always, even to the end of the age."
-Matthew 28:20 (NLT)

Don't miss the Messiah.

You've probably heard the Christmas story before.
But, have you heard about all the people mentioned in
the Bible who completely missed out on the miracle of
Jesus' birth?

There's the Innkeeper for one. Jesus literally could
have been born in his house but he sent Mary and
Joseph out to the barn instead. Then there's King
Herod who, upon hearing a religious king was born,
felt jealous instead of joyous and wiped out every boy
baby in order to save his throne. This last one is the
real shocker. The high priests and religious experts
even missed God coming to earth. Despite knowing all
the scriptures, prophesies, and exactly where the
Christ was to be born, they never even went to see if
he had come.

Who didn't miss Jesus? The culturally insignificant
shepherds, some wise men from the East, an old man,
Simeon, and an old widow named Anna.

The most unexpected, distant, outcast, forgotten
people experienced the miracle of the Messiah. Why?
Because, they were looking for it.

I'm sure almost everyone who missed Jesus' birth had

an excuse: The hustle and bustle of everyday life, the human tendency to live in ignorance instead of the Truth, or a disbelief that God could have actually interceded in our world.

Today, we miss out on encounters with Jesus for the same reasons. Humanity hasn't changed so much and God hasn't changed at all. So, if you really want to see Jesus you must do what those who found Him did - look for Him. Jesus came then, he's still here now, and he promises to never leave.

Journal or Doodle:

Have you ever missed out on an opportunity to encounter Jesus? What was the reason? How can you be intentional about looking for Jesus today and every day?

46. A City on a Hill

"You are the light of the world. A city set on a hill cannot be hidden..."
-Matthew 5:14 (ESV)

You're not alone in your loneliness.

An epidemic of disconnection is sweeping through our world. More American young adults than ever are leaving the church after high school and not rejoining a religious community. College students are reporting that, even being surrounded by thousands of other peers on a daily basis, they feel depressed and alone. Because isolation is creating social issues across the world, the first ever Minister of Loneliness was elected in the U.K.

People are growing up without family and friend connections. We're having constant text message conversations but never any face to face dialogue. We've become so good at being the social media versions of ourselves that we've forgotten how to be real with others.

I have the radical belief that you can reverse the isolation in your generation. I know for a fact that you can change the world with authentic connection. Want to hear how?

Become what Matthew 5:14 tells us to be, a city on a hill.

Cities are bright and busy. They're made up of tons of people, activities and options. They are gathering places, event locations and exciting places to visit. If they're on a hill, there's absolutely no way you could miss them.

The world is a dark place. It seems to be growing darker with loneliness by the minute. However, if we'll turn the light on and invite people into our lives, we can easily dismantle isolation by creating community right where we are.

Journal or Doodle:

What is the best thing about your favorite city? What are some ways you can create and connect to community in your environment? List 5 people you could invite to be a part of the "city" God is leading you to form or join.

47. Edging God Out

"Keep this Book of the Law always on your lips; meditate on it day and night, so that you may be careful to do everything written in it. Then you will be prosperous and successful."
-Joshua 1:8 (NIV)

In this new age world we've really started reverting back to ancient traditions. One fad that has resurfaced is meditation. Did you know meditation is Biblical? Joshua 1:8 tells us to meditate on scripture so much that we become obedient to it. Did you catch the promise at the end? *"Then you will be prosperous and successful."*

Sounds good to me! So, I decided to start making this a practice by reading the Bible at night and quietly dwelling on it. The first time I chose a guided meditation and clicked on one about fear.

"Fear is not yourself, it is your self-perception. Your ego, E.G.O. Which is another way to say 'Edging God Out.'" A voice as smooth as butter cut through me.

Suddenly, I became keenly aware of my body. The way it felt to sit on that mat…. tense, almost to the bone. I tried to gather up the courage to intentionally relax each muscle, vertebrae, and thought. I decided to stop edging God out and allow him to come uncomfortably close.

It is so easy, in an attempt to control our lives, to grab onto our ego instead of letting go. We tense up and brace ourselves against life instead of relaxing into what God is doing and breathing into the hard places. We try to drown out the noise with more noise instead of becoming silent enough to deal with it. Our natural tendency is to 'Edge God Out' because it's uncomfortable at first to let him and his Word in.

However, when we get quiet enough to become aware of what's going on in our mind, we may find it's a little scary and noisy in there. We can silence the chatter with God's truth by reading the Bible and truly meditating on it. There, in the quiet and stillness, hidden in the unexpected places of our minds and souls, might be the answers we're looking for.

Journal or Doodle:

Take time today to meditate on scripture. Choose a verse, read it, and sit with it for about two minutes. What did God say to you through his Word? Did you notice any thoughts arise that tried to distract you? If they're not in line with scripture, how can you trump the lies hidden in your heart with God's Truth?

48. The Future for Us All

"For the LORD your God is God of gods and Lord of
lords, the great God, mighty and awesome, who shows
no partiality and accepts no bribes."
-Deuteronomy 10:17 (NIV)

We're living in a #TheFutureIsFemale movement
culture. As Christian women, where should we stand?
Whose side is God on? Where does that leave us?

I once read a quote on Instagram that said, *"Teach
your daughters to worry less about fitting into glass
slippers and more about shattering glass ceilings."*

It made me recall my years when I played dress up
and wanted to be a Disney "princess." I always had to
be Pocahontas or Mulan, mainly because they couldn't
bother with small slippers. They had bigger things to
worry about - like saving nations and tribes. They
were fighters. They pushed the boundaries. They
risked their lives for their cause.

I think there, in the trunk with the Indian and Chinese
warrior costumes, are our answers. We are to simply
make it evident in today's culture that we are God's
daughters who dress for their futures in the same
way. Seeing the feminine fighter within. Battling for
not only women's equality, but for people to become
unified on the level ground at the foot of the cross.
Believing in ourselves, God, and passions. Seeing only
the fullest life, not the limitations that may be placed
on us from others.

The future isn't only female, but also male. It's red,

yellow, black and white. It's the rich and poor. It's diverse and shared across the universe. If God shows no partiality, there is a hope and future for all who will accept it.

Journal or Doodle:

What are some of the greatest tensions in today's American culture? As a young woman, where do you think God wants you to stand? How does it make you feel to know God offers a future and hope for us all?

49. Our Daily Bread

"This, then, is how you should pray: "'Our Father in heaven, hallowed be your name, your kingdom come, your will be done, on earth as it is in heaven. Give us today our daily bread. And forgive us our debts, as we also have forgiven our debtors. And lead us not into temptation, but deliver us from the evil one.'"
-Matthew 6:9-13 (NIV)

"This day our daily bread."

This is the hardest part of the Lord's Prayer for us to really, genuinely live out in the Wander years. We have an unknown future. The most common question we're asked is "What are you going to do next?"

So, we read this and want to yell back, "But what about tomorrow?" "What if this only gets worse?" "What if that past mistake plagues me in the future?"

Somewhere along the way, life taught us to self-preserve, prepare for the worst and let our past dictate our future.

However, this lifestyle has us so concerned about creating tomorrow that we miss out on what blessings God has given us today. Instead of taking in our daily portion of "what is" we're reaping the spoils of "what if."

Fear is preparing for tomorrow with a doomsday mentality. Freedom is portion control. It is daily bread because life is best lived in the present, savored in contentment and full of hope for the future.

<u>Journal or Doodle:</u>

Do you find yourself dwelling more on "what if" or
"what is?" What blessings has God given you in the
present and how can you best savor them today? Take
time to pray now for daily bread, for today's needs to
be met, thanking God for all he's doing right now in
this moment.

50. What Is Rest?

"... He said to them, "Come with me by yourselves to a quiet place and get some rest."
-Mark 6:31 (NIV)

There's a saying that goes something like, "Healthy bodies need movement, and healthy minds need stillness." This is incredibly hard when we have a whole other world at our finger tips through our phones. When we're not looking down at our devises there's usually homework answers to look up or a side job, club or sport vying for our attention. What is rest? How can we find it in a society that praises busyness?

Mark 6:31 gives us three culture defying clues we can do in five minutes:

1. "Come with me by yourselves..." We have to disconnect to reconnect to our souls. So, take one minute to turn your phone on airplane mode and bury it in your bag. Forget your calendar and homework momentarily. Go find a place to be alone for just a bit and take in your surroundings, your life, without distraction.

2. "A quiet place." I remember the first time I meditated it sounded like my mind was playing a movie in fast forward. I had no idea there was so much noise in there until it was quiet enough to hear it! You try the same thing. Be absolutely quiet. Just for about three minutes. Observe your thoughts without participating in them. Scan yourself from the tip of your head down to your toes. How does your body and mind really feel? What's in your head and heart?

What's a Bible verse you can quote over memories, sensations, lies or strong emotions that arise?

3. "Get some rest." When we've taken the time to allow our souls catch up to our busy bodies, we can finally, truly rest. After disconnecting and mediating, we may want to stay in this quiet place for a while. Or we may have another activity to rush off to. But five minutes of rest is better than no rest at all and we'll be so grateful for anything we can get.

Just try this three-step rest today. Maybe disconnecting will create the reconnection with God you've been seeking all along.

<u>Journal or Doodle:</u>

After trying the three-step rest, did you notice any change? What is God teaching you about resting in him today?

Tell God your "I don't knows" and allow him to reply with his "I do's."

AS YOU WANDER

51. Come on Home

"God's a safe-house for the battered, a sanctuary during bad times. The moment you arrive, you relax; you're never sorry you knocked."
-Psalm 9:9-10 (MSG)

It was the greatest cross-country road trip of our lives. We had gone from Colorado to Vegas and then all the way down Highway 1. Once we got to LA, we figured we'd book it on home.

We'd been camping across the country now for weeks. We were dirty. We wanted real food. And more than anything, we wanted a bed.

So, we started driving and, being past the point of delirium, we just kept driving. In fact, we drove straight from LA to South Carolina. Yes, 48 hours of driving.

Finally reaching home, we got out of the car and practically kissed the ground. We ran up to the room, no showers, no real food, and just plopped down into the bed. The fluffy sheets and the soft pillow enveloped us and this felt like heaven.

Nothing. I mean nothing, ever felt so good!

This is what it's like to enter into God's house when you've been gone for a while. You're a Wanderer so you've journeyed down some dusty, bumpy roads in life. You've laid your head in places and situations that you may regret. You feel dirty and hungry and all you want is to come home.

Here's the good news! You can pack up and go to that safe haven. At God's place, the light is always on. He has a bed made up just for your weary head. This sanctuary is waiting for you to come kick your feet up and relax.

So, if you've been gone for a while from God's presence. Come on home.

Journal or Doodle:

Have you ever been gone from home for a while and couldn't wait to get back to the comfort of your own place? What is it like when you haven't experienced God's presence for a while and decide to make time and space to come back? What does God's house look and feel like to you?

52. God's Love Language

"So be very careful to love the Lord your God."
-Joshua 23:11 (NIV)

Have you ever heard the term "love languages?"

Basically, it's how you like to give and receive love.

Author Gary Chapman wrote a book about this called "The Five Love Languages." In it he says, *"I would encourage you to make your own investigation of the one whom, as He died, prayed for those who killed Him: 'Father forgive them for they know not what they do.' That is love's ultimate expression."*

There's a lot of talk about how God loves us, but has it ever occurred to you that God likes to be loved too?

There's a very simple way to love on God. Think about the ways that you like to be cared for, and do that to show God how much you care.

If you like to receive love letters, write out your next prayer. If hanging out with your friends makes you feel accepted, try spending five minutes every day talking to God. Do you feel appreciated when a family member does a chore for you or cooks your favorite meal? Then sign up to serve at your local church or an organization in your community.

Joshua 23 sets the reminder to *"be very careful to love the Lord"* because it's easy to forget to do. God's going to love you no matter what. Let him know that matters to you.

Journal or Doodle:

How do you like to give and receive love? What are you love languages? How can you show God you love him today?

53. Run Your Race

"Therefore, since we are surrounded by such a great cloud of witnesses, let us throw off everything that hinders and the sin that so easily entangles. And let us run with perseverance the race marked out for us, fixing our eyes on Jesus, the pioneer and perfecter of faith."
-Hebrews 12:1-2 (NIV)

"Finish strong." Have you ever heard this phrase? I don't know about you, but it's one of the hardest things for me to do. Most of the time, when I'm at the tail end of something, I'm just ready to wrap things up and move on.

However, Hebrews 12:1-2 tells us that life is a race. It doesn't specify what kind, but let's assume it's not a sprint because it's laid out that we're going to need some perseverance. This isn't a "give it all you've got and give up when it's gone" way of living. This is finding a way to keep running, consistently, all the way to the finish line.

So how to do we finish strong when we're tempted to end weak?

1. **Fix your focus**- Christine Caine puts it this way, *"Some of you aren't running your race because you're too busy scrolling through everyone else's."* Stop swiping through social media to rival your speed, attire, and abilities to the people next to you. This isn't their race, it's yours. Set your eyes on your own God-given talents and go with them, as fast as you can, out into the world.

2. **Love your lane-** What do you love to do? Babysit? Host Bible studies? Talk about astrophysics, solve world hunger, or sing carpool karaoke? Doing what you love is God's calling for you and will inspire you to end well. If you're lagging a few steps before the finish line, it's because you don't love your lane. Rediscover your passions and re-fire your pursuit.

3. **Find your finish-** Hebrews 12:1 talks about a "great cloud of witnesses" to remind us that we're not alone. Like a rowdy student section at a football game, all believers are cheering us on in our faith race to the very end. Listen to their voices, be encouraged by their advice, and lean on them when you're tired. You'll find the finish line isn't quite so hard to reach when you discover the great footsteps you're following in.

Finish strong, Wanderers, because the way you wrap up this season will determine how the next one unfolds.

Journal or Doodle:

What season of life is wrapping up for you right now? What steps can you take to ensure that you finish strong?

54. Live What You've Learned

"Your love for one another will prove to the world that you are my disciples."
-John 13:35 (NLT)

The Bible says that faith without works is dead (James 2:17). Meaning, it's time to live what you've learned.

If we're living proof of God's love, we have some awesome responsibilities: like making friends, helping others in need, and being a part of someone else's story.

The challenge for you today is to find a simple way to love. Here are four ideas:

1. Send an encouraging text to your friends or Bible study group.
2. Sit with someone who typically sits alone at lunch. Get to know them.
3. Say, "I'm praying for you" and mean it. Text them later a summary of your prayer.
4. Perform a random act of kindness, like buying someone their favorite snack during class break or taking care of a chore for your mom or roommate without being asked.

Let's tell the world today about Jesus by simply shining His love into a dark world that so desperately needs it.

Journal or Doodle:

How can you love someone else today? What do you
expect God to do through you as you live out his
Word? Pray, tell him your expectations, and ask him to
use you in a great way.

55. Show the Best, Hide the Rest

"I form the light and create darkness, I make peace and create calamity; I, the LORD, do all these things.'"
-Isaiah 45:7 (ESV)

As social media is taking the world by storm, it's sweeping up the church with it. What I fear is that we are teaching your generation to be avatars and not actual people. To reveal only the good stuff and tuck the bad part of your life into a deleted folder. To show the best and hide the rest.

I want you to know the truth: We are not a summation of only the most awesome things that have ever happened to us, but a funky blend of all the light and darkness in our lives. To be authentic believers and grow in our relationship with Christ, we have to stop setting a social media standard for faith and start getting real about our lives. Something has to change, but what?

What isn't going to change is people posting pictures of only good things. Because, who wants to view a photo of themselves crying on their worst day? That time we fell in the school parking lot in front of all the senior boys? (You laugh but this really happened to me). The dregs of coffee? No. We as humans enjoy lovely things and will never stop wanting to immortalize what's beautiful. However, what we can alter is the assumption that only the best moments define our lives.

As we interact with others, remember our contacts may have thousands of followers but it doesn't mean they don't feel lonely. Our friend's constant need to post selfie photos might not be a stance of confidence but an outcry of insecurity. The popular kid who has edited their photos down to a perfect science might be trying to edit out some brokenness that God wants to use in their life to bring wholeness.

So, go a little deeper than just talking to your peers about the Instagram worthy things. Dig deep and find out how someone really is.

Don't just get to know someone's best. Let them know that God loves the rest of their story too.

Journal or Doodle:

Do you think you have to reveal only the best side of yourself? What does it mean that God loves and wants to use the rest of your life too? How might that impact the way you see and interact with others?

56. The Curtain and the Cross

"We have this hope as an anchor for the soul, firm and secure. It enters the inner sanctuary behind the curtain, where our forerunner, Jesus, has entered on our behalf."
-Hebrews 6:19-20.(NIV)

My mom always had big Kirkland's looking curtains in our living room. The pretty, embroidered type with tassels that sit in display windows.

This is the curtain I pictured each time that I read the story of Jesus dying for our sins on the cross where the Bible says, *"At that moment the curtain of the temple was torn in two from top to bottom* (Matthew 27:51)."

However, this carried more weight than anyone ever told me. Literally. It was 60 feet high, 30 feet wide and four inches thick. This curtain is also referred to as a "veil" which translated to Hebrew is screen or divider. This was not a Kirkland's curtain. This was a beautifully crafted wall that guarded a sacred secret.

The curtain-wall divided the rest of the world from the Holy of Holies, the space in the temple where God's presence dwelled on earth. Permitted to be visited by the high priest only after he had perfectly prepared himself, this curtain wall insured that consecrated, holy things were let in and all the flawed, sinful stuff was kept out.

That means you and I were out. We couldn't just walk into the temple like we do our church. We couldn't experience God's presence like we now do in great times of worship and prayer. Our sin was so thick and heavy it divided us from a relationship with God.

However, when Jesus died, he took our sin to the grave and exposed the secret of life in God's presence. He unleashed Love on the earth that was unlike anything we'd ever seen and nothing could separate it from us. There was no more curtain-wall!

The veil was *"torn in two from top to bottom* (Matthew 27:51)." There is no going back, no stitching that thing back together. The whole earth has become entirely exposed to the Holy of Holies. Hallelujah! We forever have complete access to the presence of God through Jesus!

Journal or Doodle:

Have you ever taken the access you have to the presence of God for granted? What does it mean to you that, through Jesus' death and resurrection, we all now have total access to a holy God?

57. God Has It

"For God gave us a spirit not of fear but of power and love and self-control."
-2 Timothy 1:7 (ESV)

My name is Kaley and I have anxiety.

Notice, I didn't say anxiety has me.

It's easy to believe, when we're anxious or depressed that we're out of control. We tend to think that we've done something to deserve this. We buy into the lie that we're meant to survive with mental weakness instead of thrive in the fullness of life.

Here's the truth.

The Bible says we are more powerful than our problems, have a sound mind and can take our thoughts captive. God's love will quiet all our fears, and we have a future full of hope. Christ died that we may live our life to the brim, not just half full or empty.

Dr. Caroline Leaf puts it this way, *"We must continually monitor what passes through our five senses. Whatever you think about will grow and what you grow is what you do."*

What thought patterns we allow our mind to practice are the patterns we give power to. So, let's grow healthy thoughts. Let's turn up the volume on God's truth and cut down the lies that we tend to tell ourselves.

Whatever you have, remember that God has it too. Right there in the palm of His hand.

Journal or Doodle:

Follow up today's reading by checking out these verses: 2 Timothy 1:7, 2 Corinthians 10:5, Zephaniah 3:17, and Jeremiah 29:11. Write down the lies you currently believe about your life and the truths you find in these scriptures beside them. How can these verses remind you of your God-given strength where you feel mentally weak?

58. Heart Surgery

"In the same way, the Spirit helps us in our weakness. We do not know what we ought to pray for, but the Spirit himself intercedes for us through wordless groans. And he who searches our hearts knows the mind of the Spirit, because the Spirit intercedes for God's people in accordance with the will of God."
-Romans 8:26-27 (NIV)

I spent my sophomore year spring break in a hospital. Why? My dad, my hero, my first visible form of incarnated strength and faith, was being cut open. His life was completely vulnerable to the hands of a surgeon. Despite the graphic image, there was something beautiful about this situation.

The surgeon warned our family that after open-heart surgery, Dad might become more emotional than usual. If the human heart is physically touched, we can become prone to depression, sadness and deep emotion.

Isn't it interesting how our physical and spiritual hearts are so connected?

While you may not have had open-heart surgery, you have had something touch your heart. An encouraging word. Love returned from people you care about. An unexpected gift. Or you have even had something break your heart. The loss of a relationship. A dream crushed. An insult.

God is always in the process of healing our hearts, so what can help us deal with the pain in the process?

For my dad's recovery after surgery, the doctors gave him a pillow to squeeze when he had to cough or felt chest pains. That's exactly what God does for us when we need help! He gives us something that can act as a cushion between our hearts and hurts when we feel weak and need comfort.... The HOLY SPIRIT!

Romans 8:26-27 says, *"The Spirit helps us in our weakness."* Like the doctors gave my dad something for pain and comfort, Jesus gifted the Holy Spirit to us when he ascended up to heaven so that we would have a helper here on earth. We can grab on to the Holy Spirit, cry out in pain and find comfort during the healing of our hurting hearts.

Journal or Doodle:

What are some things, good or bad, that have deeply touched your heart? How can you hold on to the Holy Spirit and let God help you heal?

59. Someone Else's Rain Boots

"Praise be to the God and Father of our Lord Jesus Christ, the Father of compassion and the God of all comfort, who comforts us in all our troubles, so that we can comfort those in any trouble with the comfort we ourselves receive from God."
-2 Corinthians 1:3-4 (NIV)

I once read an awesome quote that said, *"Do not judge. You do not know what storm I've asked her to walk through. – God."*

It resonated with me so much because the longer I'm in ministry the more I realize that it's not my place to judge the size of anyone's storm. What might seem like an easy drizzle for me to walk through might be a downpour for a sister that can't seem to find the sunlight.

So, when people tell you their problems, spill their guts to you about a hurricane that's wrecking their lives, don't blow them off by saying, "Ah, you'll get through this" or "It's not THAT bad." Here's why - to them this wind and rain will never relent. To them it is THAT bad.

If we really and genuinely want to help others, we have to start walking a mile in someone else's rain boots. We've got to open up our umbrellas, grab a sister's hand while she's getting drenched, and walk beside her. The reality is that sometimes people don't need your judgment or advice, they just need a friend.

Journal or Doodle:

Have you ever tried to help someone and ended up hurting them instead? What does it mean to be an authentic friend? Who is someone God has called you to stand beside through their rainy season? How can you pray for them?

60. How to Hear from God

"For since the creation of the world God's invisible qualities - his eternal power and divine nature - have been clearly seen, being understood from what has been made, so that people are without excuse."
-Romans 1:20 (NIV)

It's hard to follow a God we can't see and listen to a God we can't hear. We wish Jesus would show up in person to save us from our problems. It would be so much easier to make a decision if he would just yell at us from heaven which way to go.

There's a song by Sean McConnell, "Madly in Love With You" that says,

"I know you wish you could see me
That's the way it has to be
Someday you will understand
Don't you lose your faith in me.

I know you wish you could hear me
Sometimes it's so hard to do
But every morning the sunrise says
I'm madly in love with you."

Maybe we're not seeing or hearing God in our lives because we're looking for him in the wrong places. We're seeking a person and listening for a voice but he's really showing up in a sunrise and speaking to us through the wind.

Looking at nature can help us see God when it's unnatural.

If you feel like God is distant, go outside. He's handing you a bouquet of flowers. He's washing you white as snow. He's whispering to you in the rain.

Journal or Doodle:

Is God far away from you or quiet? How can you see and hear him in nature? What do you think he's showing you and saying to you?

Authentic sisterhood is accepting each other's quirks and flaws, trusting in the God who calls us all beautiful just as we are.

AS YOU WANDER

61. P.U.S.H.

"But I tell you this--though he won't do it for friendship's sake, if you keep knocking long enough, he will get up and give you whatever you need because of your shameless persistence."
-Luke 11:8 (NLT)

I grew up in a church that used a lot of acronyms.

There was the infamous "W.W.J.D." or "What would Jesus do?" I was given a bracelet from our youth group with "F.R.O.G." stamped across it standing for "Fully rely on God." The one that stuck with me the most is "P.U.S.H." meaning, "Pray until something happens."

"P.U.S.H." is the attitude that activates our prayers. Luke 11:8 calls it "shameless persistence." In other words, we need to be praying with perseverance, persistence, swagger, and boldness.

I guess the old adage "the squeaky wheel gets the grease" is a bit true in our prayer life.

We need to have enough endurance to keep praying and trust that God hears and is helping us, even when we can't see it.

Perseverance in prayer is probably one of the hardest things because we want to see answers on earth and God wants to see growth in heaven. But, like the neighbor in Luke 11 that kept knocking and relentlessly asking, we can know that if we come to God, even in the darkest hour of desperation, He will give us exactly what we need.

Journal or Doodle:

What persevering prayers are you tempted to give up
on? How can you find fresh inspiration for your old
requests?

62. Daughter for Sale

"...The prayer of the person living right with God is something powerful to be reckoned with. Elijah, for instance, human just like us, prayed hard that it wouldn't rain, and it didn't- not a drop for three and a half years. Then he prayed that it would rain and it did. The showers came and everything started growing again."
-James 5:16 (MSG)

Coffee is my lifeline. It is the reason I slump out of bed in the morning and the cause of my sustained consciousness throughout the day. Can I get an "Amen?" So, at this hour, you better believe I'm sipping on a cup at my desk. But I read my first email of the morning about the Horn of Africa and it makes me forget I have taste...

"A Reuter's story today highlights a new practice affecting young girls in the area, "drought brides." Some desperate parents are making the choice to sell one of their daughters in marriage in order to have enough money to buy food for their other children. The average price for these girls - some as young as 10 - is about $150."

Can you imagine being sold by your parents for food? Standing in the shoes of the drought bride, what would it be like to look into the eyes of someone you do not love but realizing you had to give yourself in order for your family to eat? They're starving and life is something money can't buy. What if you were only 10 years old...?

Take a few moments today and just sit in silence. Take off your watch. Go to a secret place and talk to God. Picture yourself in the shoes of another, whether that be the drought bride, a starving child overseas, a natural disaster victim, the homeless man down the road, or maybe even just a hurting friend. Pour your heart out on their behalf. And, like James 5:16 says, do not underestimate the power of prayer.

Journal or Doodle:

Whose shoes did you put yourself in as you prayed? What did it feel like to be them? Did God speak anything specifically to your heart? How can you continue to think of and pray for others?

63. Create Fewer Deserts

"My beloved is to me a cluster of henna blossoms from the vineyards of En Gedi."
-Song of Solomon 1:14

I loved Mexico. Palm trees folding over a bleached shoreline laced with the foam of a gemstone ocean. Sun-soaked skin and no obligations to do anything except to tan a little longer. Peace and tranquility ... until the plane lands, my phone uploads, and emails and texts come rolling in.

Responsibility hits like a tropical storm after a time of rest and relaxation. So, what's the balance between work and play? How can we stay refreshed when it seems like our daily responsibilities threaten to drain us?

Go back to Mexico! I'm only kidding. Sort of. We have a place kind of like that. A place we can travel to, no matter where we are. A place called En Gedi.

En Gedi is an oasis in a desert. It's a place of rest, renewal, and refuge. Finding it requires two things.

1. Care for ourselves.
Giving our time away, even doing noble things like church or school, can deplete our energy and steal our passion. God invites us to refuel by doing the things we love. Take a nap. Read the Bible. Go get your favorite coffee. As one of my friends puts it, "It's not selfish, if it's self-care."

2. Care for others.

We're creating either a desert or an oasis. We're overflowing with God's love or draining the life out of our relationships by our selfishness and self-centeredness. We can truly, deeply care for others by giving without an expectation of getting something in return.

Be intentional. Find your En Gedi. Remain with Jesus in this refuge - this restful, safe place - in the midst of the harsh world around you.

Journal or Doodle:

On a scale of 1 to 10 (1 being terrible and 10 being awesome) how good are you at taking care of yourself? On the same scale, how intentional are you about caring for others? What do you need to change to create En Gedi in your environment?

64. I Don't Know

"The heart of man plans his way,
but the Lord establishes his steps."
-Proverb 16:9 (ESV)

"Where are you going to college?"
"Have you decided on a major?"
"What are you going to do when you graduate?"

I remember questions about the future seeming
relentless and my answer always staying the same.
"Look people... I DON'T KNOW!!"

What a very unpopular answer. We celebrate the five-
year plans and resume builders but that tends to leave
a lot of us in the "fail" zone doesn't it? We are ashamed
that we are changing our major... again. We applied to
five colleges and now we don't know how to choose
the right one. We're going to graduate soon and the
job applications are out there but we still haven't
heard anything back. The future seems so bright
sometimes that we're blinded by it.

I recently discovered some great news for all of us "I-
Don't-Knowers." You ready? We don't have to know
and sometimes we're not even supposed to! When we
can't tell God exactly what we want, we've actually
created a ton of space for him to tell us what he wants
for us.

So, tell God your "I don't knows" and allow him time to
reply with his "I do's." Focus your prayers on listening
for direction instead or asking for your way. Then, as

you make your future plans, you can rest in knowing the Lord will direct every shaky step.

Journal or Doodle:

Have you ever had an "I don't know" answer to a big future question? How did God answer with his plans and come through for you? How does this assure you of how he'll come through for you in times of uncertainty for the future?

65. Pull the Ripcord

"God can't break his word. And because his word cannot change, the promise is likewise unchangeable. It's an unbreakable spiritual lifeline, reaching past all appearances right to the very presence of God."
-Hebrews 6:18-19 (MSG)

"Ripcord." That's what Carowinds theme park accurately named the ride that hoists you 150 feet in the air, face down, and crammed next to your best friends in nothing but a harness.

Growing up just a short drive from Carowinds made me do a few crazy things as a teenager and this was one of them. I remember looking at my friends standing in line on that day we were finally brave enough to ride. My heart was screaming in my chest as we got to the top and I looked down, palms sweating, at the giant target a world away on the ground. The moment I pulled the ripcord that sent us free falling toward the earth, I grabbed onto my harness like my life depended on it. Why? Because, it did.

Being held is being free.

It makes no sense. Letting go and total independence means freedom, right?

Sometimes we want to wiggle out of our restraints and pull the ripcord on our lives. We don't want God to hold us back from anything, our parents to tell us what to do, or the rules established in the Bible to keep us from the excitement of life. However, just like the harness, God and his Word are protection from smacking rock bottom. When we fall, he catches us.

So, freedom isn't the absence of restraint, it's really the presence and nearness of God and love. It's there that we're safe enough to finally let go and fall knowing we're going to get picked back up again. It's being wild and totally free.

Freedom isn't letting go, it's holding on as tightly as we can. It isn't finding our own space in the world, it's sharing our space with the world. It isn't becoming who we are on our own, it's coming close and learning who God created us to be.

Journal or Doodle:

Did you ever experience a theme park ride that made you cling onto your harness or seat? What if you held on that tightly to God and his Word? How does it shift your perspective on God's "rules" knowing they're there to protect you, not prevent you from having fun?

66. You Can Do Hard Things

"So when Jesus had received the sour wine, He said, 'It is finished!' And bowing His head, He gave up His spirit."
-John 19:30 (ESV)

Why are we so afraid of hard things?

We assume that because it's tough, God isn't in it. Because this time is dark or painful, it must be Satan. It's a consequence. A burden. A pain.

However, the Bible calls Jesus a man of sorrows. Well acquainted with grief and pain and rejection (Isaiah 53:3). Over 2,000 years ago he was unjustly put on trial for crimes he didn't do, undeservingly beaten for a law he never broke, and unashamedly hung on a cross for sins he hadn't committed.

The result of living in a broken world is that bad things happen. The good news of Good Friday is that Jesus was broken for our brokenness.

While this may be the hardest thing we have ever walked through, darkest night, or most painful situation, we worship a God who not only understands but is well acquainted with our sorrow, rejection, and even death.

C.S. Lewis put it this way, *"God whispers to us in our pleasures, speaks in our conscience, but shouts in our pains."*

We can endure bad, hard things because our Jesus overcame the world with Satan's best attempt at defeating it. The worst moment became the best thing to ever happen in history. So, God is often doing his best work in our worst circumstances. He is the loudest in the hardest problems. He is closest in our deepest pain.

Don't complain so much that you miss the intimacy of the cross. It is the closeness of Jesus shouting, *"You're going to make it because I've already made it. You're going to overcome because look at all I overcame. You're totally accepted because I was rejected, adopted because I was cast out, and free because I paid it all. Your life can begin because 'it is finished."*

Journal or Doodle:

In hardship, do you find yourself complaining and pushing away from God? How would it change your circumstances to look at the cross and draw close to Christ knowing that he understands your hurt? Your life can begin because 'It is finished.' What does this phrase mean to you?

67. The Burial Before the Blessing

"For I passed on to you as of first importance what I also received, that Christ died for our sins according to the Scriptures, and that he was buried, and that he was raised up on the third day according to the Scriptures."
-1 Corinthians 15:3-4 (NIV)

When we talk about Jesus, we tend to focus on his resurrection. However, what about the break down before the break through? What's significant about the burial before the blessing?

After Jesus died on the cross, he was wrapped in burial clothes and placed in a tomb. For three whole days, his body stayed in the grave. Yup, he was dead alright.

However, something amazing happened that I think is best summarized by this statement by Christine Cane, *"Sometimes when you're in a dark place you think you've been buried but you've actually been planted."*

What the world didn't know about the tomb is that it couldn't hold Jesus. He defeated death and on that third day rose from the grave. This means that when we think we're stuck in our darkest situation, we're really on the brink of our greatest season of growth. The death of that dream, unhealthy relationship or expectation was hard and it hurt. However, our burial becomes our blessing when we allow God to give purpose to our placement.

Sometimes things have to die to give life to new dreams and second chances. Sometimes we have to experience the darkness so that we can see the light.

1 Corinthians 15:3-4 is proof that God is in the business of making heavens out of our hells, turning tombs into triumphs, and bringing life out of death.

If God can turn a crucifixion into a resurrection, think about all the wonderful things he's up to in your life.

Journal or Doodle:

What hopes or expectations have you had to bury in your life? What blessings have you seen come from that? If you're in the midst of a painful situation, create a prayer asking God to turn your tomb into a triumph.

68. The Weathering of Worry

"Do not be anxious about anything, but in every situation, by prayer and petition, with thanksgiving, present your requests to God."
-Philippians 4:6 (NIV)

"There is no bad weather, only bad clothes," read the wall of the camping store.

Moving to Aspen, Colorado, taught me that this is absolutely true. I started living in freezing temperatures with only the gear I had from growing up in the southern Carolina humidity - an old winter jacket and a pair of fashionably furry boots. I wasn't a minute into walking down Main Street before my clothes were sopping wet with heavy snow and I was frozen.

Worry can affect us the same way as snow in the Colorado Mountains. If we haven't put on the right gear to protect our hearts and minds, anxiety can leave us frozen, numb and miserable.

So how do we protect ourselves from the weathering of worry?

Philippians 4:6 says the best thing to put on when anxiety threatens to storm into our lives is prayer. Here are two reasons why:

1. Like a good ski jacket, if we cover ourselves in prayer, we're no longer exposed to the worst part of our situation. We don't have to handle anything alone

because there is a God who loves us and is shielding us from whatever may come our way.

2. Prayer is like trading in your old jacket and boots for some brand new gear. When we give our problems and concerns to God, He replaces them with his peace. Totally free of charge.

Worry can make our hearts grow cold. Anxiety soaks us in doubt and tries to stop us from moving forward in our faith. However, if we'll put on prayer, even our worst worry can't stop God from bringing great things out of our lives.

Journal or Doodle:

How can you protect yourself from worry and anxiety? What situations do you need to cover in prayer?

69. A Banana is not a Car Key

"Smile on me, your servant; teach me the right way to live."
-Psalm 119:135 (MSG)

In case you did not know, a banana is not a car key.

It was officially a Monday morning. I was running late to my college internship and the dash around my room and out the door left my head spinning. In an attempt at calming myself, I took a deep breath when I got into the car, exhaled, and closed my eyes.

I grabbed what I thought were my car keys and banged them into the ignition. "Why won't this stupid thing work?" Frustrated, I looked down to discover that it was my banana I was shoving into the keyhole! I grabbed it for breakfast on the marathon to my Jeep.

A belly laugh erupted out of me as stress melted into hysterics. It was a moment I wanted everyone and yet no one to know about. So, of course, I told my co-workers all about it as soon as I arrived at the office. It felt so good to cut through the stress with laughter.

The next day, I was greeted at my desk by a bright yellow banana. The thought of it made me want to tell you to smile at the silly things in life. May the joy of the Lord burst in your heart today, cut through any of your stress, and remind you that God is smiling on you too.

Journal or Doodle:

What is stressing you out the most right now? How can you make time to laugh and experience joy in the midst of your situation? How does it make you feel to know God is smiling on you?

70. How Beautiful

"How wonderful, how beautiful, when brothers and sisters get along!"
-Psalm 133:1 (MSG)

Did you know that we are beautiful when we get along with our sisters?

When we were little, my sister and I fought constantly. Our character was as opposite as our characteristics. It was very much like pulling teeth to get us to agree on anything and, when we finally did, we were so exhausted from fighting that we didn't even want to play with each other. However, something shifted as we got older.

I remember being in college and getting a phone call from her asking me for advice. After hanging up, my heart jumped for a second. We had finally grown up and found connection beyond our preferences, personality, and passions. We were actually acting like sisters! It was beautiful...

Really we're all sisters every time we laugh with the girl next to us in class, help our mom carry the groceries, and make a phone call to a friend we haven't seen in a while. We're doing something lovely when we decide to not compare ourselves to the girl shopping beside us, but instead tell her that the color of that shirt would look awesome on her instead. We're creating unity when we transform a comment of gossip into a word of encouragement. God has even given us the ability to recreate beauty by passing on the glow of graciousness, friendliness, and sisterhood to the next girl who is desperately longing to light up with connection and acceptance.

Authentic sisterhood is accepting each other's quirks and flaws, trusting in the God who calls us all beautiful just as we are. We are unified as his daughters and warriors and crowned as the leading ladies in our own God written story. No matter who we are, we can share and celebrate in this together. How beautiful is that?

Journal or Doodle:

Has a friend or sister ever extended a great effort to get along with you? What did it mean to you that they wanted you to feel accepted and loved? How can you create authentic sisterhood in the community around you?

*Before you try to throw out
the worn-out pages from
your past, remember that
everything belongs in
the story of you.*

AS YOU WANDER

71. Conviction vs. Condemnation

"So now there is no condemnation for those who
belong to Christ Jesus."
-Romans 8:1 (NIV)

There's a big difference in conviction and
condemnation. Let's sort this out because often we get
them confused.

Let's start here: What is condemnation?
Condemnation is the voice that tells you you're a
failure. That your past sins can hold you back from a
bright future. That you should settle in life because
this is as good as it's going to get.

A lot of times in our relationship with God, we allow
condemnation to slip in. It almost feels religious to
believe that we would have to earn his love and grace.
We don't think we measure up and then we give up.
We believe we deserve to be dealt a bad hand or
remain unforgiven.

However, condemnation isn't from God. Conviction is.

So, what is conviction? Conviction is when we want to
be close to God even though we've wandered away. It
makes us fall on our knees when we've let God down
so that he can lift us back up again. It's when we're so
moved by perfect love that we grow through our
imperfections.

Know this! If we belong to Christ Jesus, accepting his
free gift of salvation through his death and

resurrection, then we are not ever condemned. Condemnation isn't from God but conviction is evidence of the God you stand for. So, stop living a life in bondage to guilt because by grace you have been set free for eternity.

Journal or Doodle:

Do you ever get condemnation and conviction confused? What do you think is the biggest difference between the two?

Take a moment to identify an area of guilt in your life and ask God to wash it away with his grace. Now, find something you are convicted about and pray that he will show you what steps you need to take to grow through your imperfections. Write down anything that comes to mind.

72. Hiking Partner

"And God said, "I will be with you. And this will be the sign to you that it is I who have sent you: When you have brought the people out of Egypt, you will worship God on this mountain."
-Exodus 3:12 (NLT)

Every hike begins with a destination in mind.

On this particular trip, our goal was a waterfall. The trail was marked difficult. It was completely up hill. There were ropes, ladders and boulders.

About half way up, I heard a loud crack underneath my right heel. I panicked as I slipped downward until my friend caught and pushed me forward onto the nearest rock. I felt so bad for falling and throwing dirt in his face. He, however, seemed unfazed as he wiped the brown flecks off his cheek and smiled to say, "It is okay, I'm not going to leave you. You can do this."

Guess what? I believed it.

His words gave me the confidence I needed to keep climbing. Up and up. Back and forth. The promise of the waterfall calling. Finally, a rushing river pounded the path before us as we overlooked the magnificent surge plummeting downward over boulders.

There is a similar danger to following God. People warn you about the level of difficulty you'll face on your journey. The climb will be great, the road will be long, and you may slip and fall a few times. The good thing about the tough trek is that the words spoken to me are the same words God encourages us all with today in Exodus 3:12, *"I will be with you."*

Who are the people God has placed on your path to support you? They could be classmates, family members, church leaders, or friends. They are God's reminder that you don't have to walk through life alone. Reach out and let them catch you when you slip up, encourage you onward toward your goals, and remind you that the struggle is worth the view from the top.

Journal or Doodle:

Who has God surrounded you with to walk beside you on your journey? What are your goals and how can you ask them to help you get there?

73. Are You Afraid of the Light?

"This is the crisis we're in: God-light streamed into the world, but men and women everywhere ran for the darkness. They went for the darkness because they were not really interested in pleasing God. Everyone who makes a practice of doing evil, addicted to denial and illusion, hates God-light and won't come near it, fearing a painful exposure. But anyone working and living in truth and reality welcomes God-light so the work can be seen for the God-work it is."
-John 3:19-21 (MSG)

I'm *that* girl. The wimpy chick who can never watch scary movies. The little child who slept with her night light on. The girl that screamed at every movement on the haunted trail.

Maybe you're *that* girl like me. Or, maybe you're brave and bold and do awesome things like sleep with all the lights off.

No matter who you are, if you're not afraid of the dark, you're afraid of the light.

We hide our sin and pride in the dark places of our lives and hearts because we have a fear of being exposed. Over time, we get used to seeing ourselves in that dim light. It deceives us into believing our life looks pretty good.

We compare by saying, *"Sure, we've messed up. But, our sin isn't as big as hers, so we're probably fine."* We dismiss our lack of discipline by thinking, *"We haven't been praying every day, but why do we need to?*

Everything is going pretty good. We don't need God right now, but we'll reach out when we do." Then, boom!

We experience heartbreak or hardship. Suddenly, the spotlight is on us. Just like when we flip on the lights after a long night's sleep, we see for the first time what we really look like. Light shines into our darkness. We realize we've messed up. We need a miracle. We need God.

John 3:19-20 is calling us to live a life wide open and invite Jesus to pierce the darkness with the Light of His love.

Whatever you've been keeping in the dark, bring it to God in his life-giving light. There's nothing to be afraid of when we have nothing to hide.

Journal or Doodle:

If you've tried to keep a secret sin, how hard was it to hold it in? What was it like when it came into the light? What does it look like for you to live a life with nothing to hide?

74. "Enough" Enough

"For all have sinned and fall short of the glory of
God, and all are justified freely by his grace through
the redemption that came by Christ Jesus."
-Romans 3:23-24 (NIV)

If I work hard enough then God will give me the future
I want. If I quit breaking his rules, he will accept me. If
I earn enough, love enough, be cool enough...

Do you ever find yourself having these thoughts? In an
achievement-based society, it makes sense to believe
that we have to earn God's love and forgiveness. I
mean, why not, that's how it works at school, home,
work, or practice. Right?

Sorry to burst your bubble, but the reality is that you
can't "enough" enough. Just read through the Ten
Commandments (Exodus 20) and you'll quickly
discover that you've broken at least one of these and
there's no way to perfectly measure up or earn your
salvation. But, that's the point!

The Bible wasn't written to make us see how badly we
don't measure up; its purpose is to show us how much
we need Jesus. We absolutely cannot follow every law
and rule perfectly but we can allow God to perfectly
love us. We can't "enough" enough, but Jesus says his
grace is enough to cover all our sin, shame, and
mistakes.

A wise friend once told me, "*Anything plus grace isn't
grace.*" The moment we try to earn God's love through
achievement, we add onto grace and take away from

the gift of salvation that Jesus freely gave us. However, when we throw up our hands in surrender and admit we need Jesus to make it through this life, we receive the raw grace that is more than we'll ever need to find freedom, forgiveness, and faith.

Journal or Doodle:

Do you ever think you don't measure up to God's expectations and find yourself trying to earn his love an acceptance? What does it look like for you to receive Jesus' gift of salvation freely? What does it mean to you that his grace is "enough?"

75. The Broken, Tattered Thing

"But he said to me, "My grace is sufficient for you, for my power is made perfect in weakness." Therefore I will boast all the more gladly of my weaknesses, so that Christ's power may rest on me."
-2 Corinthians 12:19 (NIV)

The broken, tattered things are the best! Think about your old, perfectly broken in pair of jeans, overused coffee mug with the chip in it, or picture of a loved one with the folds and fingerprints you still carry with you.

Look - sometimes we see ourselves as a broken, tattered thing. We think we're too messed up to be loved and too broken to be worthy of loving. However, the fact that we treasure shabby, unkempt things proves we don't have to be flawless to be highly valued.

This is the amazing thing about God. He loves us with our imperfections. He thinks our brokenness is beautiful. It's actually in all of those chips, cracks, and flaws that Jesus' faithfulness shines through. He uses every tear, hurt, and sin to draw us in and bring us closer to him.

So, embrace it all: every flaw and imperfection, every wound and broken place. Before you try to throw out the worn-out pages from your past, remember that everything belongs in the story of you.

Journal or Doodle:

What is your favorite broken, tattered thing? What does it mean to you that you don't have to be perfect to be perfectly loved by God?

76. Every. Single. Day.

"I discipline my body like an athlete, training it to do what it should. Otherwise, I fear that after preaching to others I myself might be disqualified."
-1 Corinthians 9:27 (NLT)

No one modeled discipline for me like Dad. Every morning I'd come down the stairs and he'd be there, eating his breakfast, sipping his coffee, reading his devotion book and Bible. Every. Single. Day.

He says it wasn't on purpose, but he'd always leave his books open there on the table after he was finished. Curiosity would get the best of me and I'd find myself sitting in his seat and, between bites of Cheerios, pouring through the pages he had just finished. Every. Single. Day.

Dad taught me through his very simple morning routine a fundamental part of my faith: Discipline is a determined decision with direct action. 1 Corinthians 9:27 parallels it to the commitment and training of an athlete. It's practicing even when you don't want to that day. It's putting in the hard work not for the instant reward, but for the long-term benefits. It's anything you do to create endurance so that you stay in the faith game.

That means, it's choosing faith over feelings, a heavenly mindset over earthly thinking, God's glory over self-entitlement, and eternal impact over instant gratification. There will be so many times in your faith journey that will be exciting and amazing. But, there will be more instances where it will be ordinary and mundane.

That's why it's called "walking with Jesus," not sprinting with him. The simple daily grind takes hard-core discipline. It's a determined decision to train to become a woman under the authority of God's Word, participate in her story, and actively share the love of Jesus in her generation. No matter what it takes. Every. Single. Day.

<u>Journal or Doodle:</u>

What does "walking with Jesus" look like and where do you feel weak in your journey? What daily discipline can you incorporate into your routine to help build endurance in that area of your faith?

77. Anticipation Leads to Celebration

"Anna, a prophet, was also there in the Temple. She was the daughter of Phanuel from the tribe of Asher, and she was very old. Her husband died when they had been married only seven years. Then she lived as a widow to the age of eighty-four. She never left the Temple but stayed there day and night, worshiping God with fasting and prayer. She came along just as Simeon was talking with Mary and Joseph, and she began praising God. She talked about the child to everyone who had been waiting expectantly for God to rescue Jerusalem."
-Luke 2:36-38 (NLT)

Have you ever applied for anything? Remember that feeling of anticipation? You complete the application process. You anxiously await the answer. Finally! A letter arrives, an email comes, or you get *the* call.

It's time to celebrate! Your wait is finally over.

That's exactly how Anna felt when Jesus showed up in the temple. Except her wait was a bit more extreme. She'd been praying for Jesus' arrival and awaiting God's answer for most of her life. Finally, the day arrived. God answered the cry of Anna's heart when Jesus showed up in the temple with His parents.

In our culture, it's hard to wait. We have smart phones, TV's, and computers. We have access to whatever we want at the click of a button. It doesn't work that way with God. His timing isn't ours. God isn't instant, he's eternal. He has a long-term plan. So, while we often want him to answer our prayers now, we have to trust that he's at work creating our best future.

Sometimes that means you don't get into the college you want or land that dream job. You don't wind up with that guy you thought you loved. On your timeline, life doesn't always pan out as planned.

Anna's life reveals that God's "not right now" doesn't mean "no." God heard her prayers, and he hears yours. He will answer them. When you are in the wait, when your best-laid plans are failing, trust that God has something better in mind. Like Anna, your anticipation will lead to celebration.

Journal or Doodle:

What plans are you making in your life right now? What do you think God's plan for your life is? How can you trust God while you wait on him to answer your prayers?

78. It's Ok to be Afraid

"Continue to work out your salvation with fear and trembling, for it is God who works in you to will and to act according to his purpose."
-Philippians 2:12 (NIV)

While we normally think fear is a bad thing, maybe Philippians 2:12 is saying that holy fear is actually an indicator of faith.

If God is working in your life, it may seem so awesome and out of your control, that it's a bit terrifying. If you're living out your salvation, the big things you feel called to do may seem a little scary.

I heard it put this way, *"Your largest fear carries your greatest growth."* That means that if you can pinpoint the thing that scares you, you can find what you're called to do. Your biggest fear is an indicator of your greatest faith. So what are you afraid of?

Are you scared of trying to restore that relationship with a parent because it failed before? Are you ignoring God's voice because you're worried about what he might say? Have you been lying to yourself because you're terrified of the consequences of admitting the truth?

When we encounter these fears, we have two choices. We can either let it paralyze us or propel us. We can either become a failure or a victor. We can ignore God or hear the hope he has to offer. We can continue to live out a lie or allow truth to set us free.

Before you throw in the towel, Philippians 2:12 says to work it out. Don't give up. Move forward through your fear because God's great will and purpose for you are just on the other side.

Journal or Doodle:

What are you afraid of and why? If you overcame it, how might your faith grow standing on the other side of your fear? What does "work out your salvation with fear and trembling" mean to you?

79. On His Shoulders

"For to us a child is born, to us a son is given, and the government will be on his shoulders. And he will be called Wonderful Counselor, Mighty God, Everlasting Father, Prince of Peace."
-Isaiah 9:6 (NIV)

As women in a nation rattled with political uncertainty, I want to remind you of what is certain. It's a promise and prophecy we read every holiday and probably never think anything about. It's used in every church play and Christmas story. Here it goes:

Isaiah 9:6 says, "...and the government will be on his shoulders."

The weight of the government is not on the president's shoulders. This verse doesn't say anything about Jesus' specific political party affiliation or what a perfect platform should look like. It doesn't tell us how to vote or where we should stand on any issues at all.

However, it does offer us some certainty and sanity about the true leader of the world. The government was placed on Jesus' shoulders thousands of years before he was born and it's been sitting there ever since. He sits higher, thinks greater, and has more control than any ruler that ever was or is to come. And, he's on your side. He votes for you and believes in all that you are and all you were created to be.

When you are bombarded with negative news headlines, relax into knowing you have a perfect ruler, Wonderful Counselor, Mighty God, Everlasting Father, and Prince of Peace. He sits on His throne above all and leads all of us with a lavish love. He carries not only the government on his shoulders, but the whole world in his hands.

Journal or Doodle:

Do news headlines and social media blasts during elections ever make you feel worried or uncertain about the political future of your country? What does it mean to you that the government actually rests on Jesus' shoulders? Stop and pray right now that your local and national government will allow Jesus to lead and God to use them.

80. The Extra Mile

"If anyone forces you to go one mile, go with them two miles."
-Matthew 5:41 (NIV)

Go the extra mile!

We've all heard this saying before. However, when it comes to loving others well, what does this really mean?

Let's back up to the origin of the phrase, which came from a time when the Jewish people were slaves to the Romans. If a Roman citizen approached a Jew and asked them for help, they had to drop what they were doing and carry whatever was asked of them for at least a mile.

So, "go the extra mile" means to surprise someone by shockingly exceeding their expectations. It's doing something hard and then something harder without being asked. It's the ice cream, whipped cream, and the cherry on top.

In your community, this looks like maximizing on opportunities to put some mind-blowing thought and effort into loving others. It's random acts of kindness. It's serving even when you're not being served. It's not just ranting about issues on social media but actually being the change you wish to see in the world.

Tune into love. Anticipate other's needs. Help carry a burden through prayer for your teacher, classmate, best friend or family without being asked. When you "go the extra mile," your relationships and their Kingdom impact grow.

Journal or Doodle:

Plan out one way you can "go the extra mile" for someone today. Come back to this page when your mission is complete and share what positive impact resulted from your actions.

It's called "walking with Jesus", not sprinting with him.

AS YOU WANDER

81. Jesus Prays For You

"Therefore he is able, once and forever, to save those who come to God through him. He lives forever to intercede with God on their behalf."
-Hebrews 7:25

Imagine for just a moment that you're standing in a prayer circle right next to Jesus. He reaches out his hand, bows his head and starts. The power of the universe rolling off his tongue in words for you. The hope of the nations is being spoken over your heart. He looks at you at the end, tears in his eyes, and says, *"You know I would've come, died on that cross, and rose again just for you. I love you."*

Man, we all could use time with Jesus like that every day as a reminder that he really is praying for us and the Holy Spirit is interceding when we don't have the words to speak.

Nineteenth century Scottish minister, Robert McCheyne boldly stated, *"If I could hear Christ praying for me in the next room, I would not fear a million enemies. Yet distance makes no difference; he is praying for me."*

So, how would you live your life differently if you could audibly hear Jesus praying for you? Would you drop all that shame and fear and move forward with full faith? Would you finally let those insecurities fall away and step up to lead confidently in all God was going to do through you? Possibly you could stop worrying about the future and start to see the miracles in the mess? You'd probably start hugging random people and letting them know they're loved because we all need that.

The fact is *"distance makes no difference."* Jesus is praying for you even if you can't hear it. So, give yourself permission to live a big life. Every day is yours. Every moment is a chance to choose your dreams over your fears. Clearly Jesus believes in you, now all you need is for you to believe in yourself.

Journal or Doodle:

What's stopping you from living the bold, brave life right now? How will you live your life differently now that you know Jesus is praying for you?

82. No Shortcuts

"Don't look for shortcuts to God. The market is flooded
with surefire, easygoing formulas for a successful life
that can be practiced in your spare time. Don't fall for
that stuff, even though crowds of people do. The way
to life - to God! - is vigorous and requires total
attention."
- Matthew 7:13-14 (MSG)

Have you ever started following your GPS only to
discover it's taking you in the wrong direction?

This is what happened to my mom when she drove to
visit me for a college scholarship interview.

"Wake Forest, NC" is what she typed into her phone as
she cranked the car engine and began her trip.
Unfortunately for her, however, Wake Forest
University isn't in Wake Forest, NC.

She thought to herself, *"Wow! This is a shorter trip
than I expected. My GPS is awesome and must have
found a better way to get there."* She just kept driving
and driving until, suddenly, she realized that she had
not found a shortcut to the university at all. Instead,
she had actually driven about two hours in the wrong
direction!

Matthew 7:13-14 tells us that the world is trying to be
our GPS. It's offering us directions to wherever we
think we should go. It's yelling at us, *"Turn here! This
way to God! Follow me!"* However, the world isn't a
good GPS because it requires us typing in the
directions. Like my mom, we often get ourselves lost.

Even worse, sometimes we don't even know where we're going.

There are no shortcuts to God. He has listed all His directions clearly for us in the Bible. Anything that points us down a different path is the wrong way to go. If we will make God our guide and let him lead the way, we'll find ourselves exactly where we were meant to be.

Journal or Doodle:

Do you feel lost or headed in the right direction right now? How can you make God the guide for your life?

83. Commonplace

"Whether you eat or drink, whatever you do, do all to the glory of God."
-1 Corinthians 10:31 (NIV)

Jesus was always commonplace and resourceful. He used ordinary stuff like water and wine (John 2:1-11), towels and dirty feet (John 13:1-17), and a little boy with his lunch box (Mark 6:30-44) to do extraordinary things.

This means that the pressure is off to find a grand situation to share the love of Christ. Or to make "drop the mic" statements every time you offer a word of encouragement or wisdom.

It also means that God can show up in the mundane. Like while we're studying, having coffee with our friends, and at our next meeting or sports practice.

Really, at its core, love is simple. It's just showing up in the normal, looking for God where he is, and joining him in it. It's seeing him in the little things and letting him do big things with them.

Pay careful attention today to God in the simple and possibly, you too, will find the miracle in the mundane.

Journal or Doodle:

Have you ever witnessed God do something awesome at an unexpected time or place? What ordinary objects and conversations will you allow God to do extraordinary things through today?

84. God Doesn't Give Up

"Have I not commanded you? Be strong and courageous. Do not be afraid; do not be discouraged, for the LORD your God will be with you wherever you go."
-Joshua 1:9 (NIV)

If you're like me, you grew up believing you don't quit anything. Even if you hate it or it's really hard. No matter what, you see it through.

However, as we grow, we quickly find out that everything changes. Seasons end. Places we used to thrive start holding us back. The time comes to leave good things and good friends. God has a new place he wants to take us. We don't have enough room in our schedule to keep the old and add the new.

To maintain sanity, we have to let something go. There are times when we have to quit.

So, if everything is susceptible to change, is there anything we can really count on? Because we can quit, does that mean God will too?

Absolutely not! Hear this truth - God is a friend who never changes or gives up on us. He is our Rock. When the world shakes, he is steady. He is the same yesterday, today and forever. Joshua 1:9 reminds us that he is with us and will never let anyone down who loves him.

We can count on God because no matter how uncertain life may be, he is the one sure thing.

Journal or Doodle:

How secure do you feel knowing that God will never
quit on you? How does this change the way you trust
in God?

85. Outsmart Satan

"Put on the whole armor of God, that you may be able to stand against the schemes of the devil. For we do not wrestle against flesh and blood, but against the rulers, against the authorities, against the cosmic powers over this present darkness, against the spiritual forces of evil in the heavenly places."
-Ephesians 6:11-12 (ESV)

We're under the impression that the devil is out to get us with bad, sinful things. When really, according to Ephesians 6, he's a schemer. He is studying you to find your weakness. His main objective is to distract you from your impact.

I once heard it put this way, *"If Satan can't make you bad, he'll make you busy."*

Here are three examples of what that may look like:

1. You pull up your social media account and start comparing your real life to someone else's highlight reel. Instead of living up to your God-given potential, you buy into the lie that you're not enough.

2. You really want to have a successful future, so you start building your resume and studying your life away. You stop doing things that seem less important, like going to church, maintaining healthy relationships or taking time for self-care.

3. You go to church camp or on a mission trip and it changes your life. The fire you felt upon returning home is quickly squelched when you realize your

friend group doesn't understand why you want to start living your life differently.

Here's how Satan works - He distracts us with seemingly good things so that we miss out on God's great things. He tells us that our to-do list is more important than recognizing all that Jesus has done for us. He slips in a few believable lies so that we miss out on the Bible's truth.

Don't be fooled! There's one easy way you can outsmart Satan's schemes. Ask yourself, *"Does this line up with God's Word?"* If the answer is "no" then let it go.

Journal and Doodle:

What are some ways that the devil is trying to distract you or make you busy? How can you outsmart Satan's lies with Biblical truth?

86. Fruit Not Fruits

"But the fruit of the Spirit is love, joy, peace, forbearance, kindness, goodness, faithfulness, gentleness and self-control. Against such things there is no law."
-Galatians 5:22-23 (NIV)

It's "FRUIT" not fruits.

Did you catch that? Maybe you're like me and you've heard this Bible verse a thousand times. Possibly this is your first time reading through the Biblically infamous "fruit of the spirit." When we read this verse, we tend to see all fruit as separate entities.

So, let's go back to the top. "But the fruit of the Spirit is..." Yep, that's fruit singular not plural. So, you can't be full of love and lack peace. You can't be kind but not faithful.

That means we're either all or none. We're either showing some growth from the Son or remaining stubbornly locked up in the bud of our self.

I've been pruning a lot of plants lately in preparation for a new season. It's a lot of cutting back, watering, and waiting. It may take months for anything to sprout from one of the branches I've trimmed or succulents I've divided.

This pruning process is what we have to undergo to grow the fruit of the Spirit. That means when you're hurt by something God has cut out or taken away from you, remember that he isn't dividing your blessings.

He's multiplying them. Your life isn't waning away, your character is developing and you're in waiting for the beginning of better, more beautiful things.

Let's let love, joy, peace, forbearance, kindness, goodness, faithfulness, gentleness and self-control all take root in our lives and see what beautiful, healthy, fresh things God can grow.

Journal or Doodle:

Does it seem like God is cutting something or someone you've loved out of your life? Has he ever done that to you in the past? How do you or did you see the fruit of the Spirit growing in you through that? What does it look like for you to come out of the bud of yourself and continue to let the Son grow you?

87. Crushed

"He anointed us, set his seal of ownership on us, and put his Spirit in our hearts as a deposit, guaranteeing what is to come."
-2 Corinthians 1:21-22 (NIV)

This has been a PRESSING season. "God is just pushing in on all those squishy sides of you," as my counselor put it.

But I'm realizing that this isn't just pressing, it's anointing. In most cases Biblically, anointing used oil. An olive had to be pressed. Wrung out completely. The vital separated and the unnecessary thrown away.

So, we can always tell where God is anointing us because that's the place he's pressing in on us most.

The hurt from that heartache is crushing. However, it will teach you how to heal a broken world. Your parent's divorce is earth shattering. But, sometimes you learn what love is by understanding what love isn't. The worst thing that's ever happened to you was absolutely that, the worst. Yet, sometimes in our darkest hour we find out just how brightly Jesus shines in our lives.

This theme of being crushed has been laid before me time and time again. Here's what I've learned: The areas you have been crushed are the arenas God has anointed you to serve out.

Journal or Doodle:

Where are you being or have you been crushed? How
has God used that pressing to pull out your passions?

88. Love One Another

"Just as I have loved you, you also are to love one another."
-John 13:34 (ESV)

Jesus' love wasn't a feel good, circumstantial kind of love. It wasn't choosy or reserved for only specific friends. The love that Jesus showed was a life-changing, boundless, never-ending, resilient, burden-bearing kind of love. It's that love that drove him to the cross, had the power to defeat the grave in his resurrection, and now brings us all from death to life.

That's the love he is commanding us to live out in John 13:34. We're charged with truly caring about others, no matter who they are or what "group" they hang out with. We're to seek out the broken hearted to heal and the forgotten to remind them they're never alone. We're supposed to be stirring up unity in a divisive culture, faith among non-believers, and trumping gossip with encouragement.

Author and pastor Max Lucado once beautifully stated, *"Let God have you, and let God love you - and don't be surprised if your heart begins to hear music you've never heard and your feet learn to dance as never before."*

Love lifts our hearts. It makes us want to dance. It completely shifts our mood and whole outlook on life. What better gift could we give to others than the perfect, life-changing love of Jesus?

If you're wondering what to do today, here's your

answer- LOVE. Truly love and you'll witness joy, authentic friendship, and answered prayers like you never have before.

Journal or Doodle:

How do you think your culture defines "love?" What does it look like for you to redefine and live out "love" this week using Jesus' example?

89. Answered Prayers Require Action

"In the same way, faith by itself, if it is not
accompanied by action, is dead."
-James 2:17 (NIV)

Have you ever prayed for something and never heard
a response from God? What if I told you that the
answer to your prayers might require action?

When Adam and Eve were hiding in shame God asked,
"Where are you (Genesis 3:9)?" When Elijah was fleeing
in fear God whispered, *"What are you doing (1 Kings
19:13)?"* To the crippled and lame Jesus healed them
and said, *"Stretch out your hand (Matt. 12:13),"* and,
"Pick up your mat (John 5:8)." To the disciples he
called, *"Come and follow me (Matt. 4:19)."* To us he
commissions, *"Go and tell (Matt. 28:19)."*

God is so powerful that he wants to empower us to
play a part in our deliverance, healing and faith. His
love is so free that he openly positions himself to be
received and allows us to come when we're ready. His
gifts are so accessible that we need only to come out
of hiding and follow him to find them.

The key to answered prayer isn't magic words,
grandiose faith or doing enough good to deserve good
things. While God could make anything happen, and
sometimes does, our prayers often require our
participation. Our answers are sometimes a result of
our actions.

God is moving toward you, so will you take a step
toward him? He's asking where you are and what

you're doing, so will you listen for his still small voice and respond? He so strongly desires your presence, so will you come? He so loves the world, so will you go?

Activate your answered prayers and be the response to someone else's requests.

Journal or Doodle:

Take a moment to pray and ask God how he wants you to participate in your prayers. What first came to your mind? What is one step you could take to activate your prayer life today?

90. Living Water in the Desert

"Therefore I am now going to allure her; I will lead her into the wilderness and speak tenderly to her."
-Hosea 2:14 (NIV)

When someone asks you to imagine the most gorgeous place you could think of, you don't typically think "desert." So, it took me by surprise how much I adored the view of my campsite in Moab, Utah. The campfire was casting shadows across dry earth; reaching up toward walls of rock only a God could build. Dirt towers were strong and stretching into the starry sky.

The desert is a place we so often find ourselves. It's where we go when we're spiritually dry, yelling out to God and hearing no answer, or chasing after our calling and consistently coming up short.

Though we rarely think we want to go into the desert, there is a beauty in this place that God wants us to discover. Hosea 2:14 says that God will sometimes actually, purposefully bring us into dry, hard, wilderness places.

A definition for "allure" according to Dictionary.com is to "make someone's mouth water." When I was in the desert I had this unquenchable thirst. I drank bottle after bottle of water with no relief. God wants us to thirst like that for Him. He is after all called the "living water (John 4:10)." When we reach deserts in life, we discover that Living Water is the only true relief in a world without fulfillment. Jesus is the only thing that can truly satisfy.

If you're in a desert, life won't always be this hard and dry. There will be a time when you escape the wilderness. Your life will be fulfilling and you will overflow. Until then, discover the beauty in the brokenness and never forget what it means to be truly desperate for Jesus.

Journal or Doodle:

Have you ever experienced a desert in life? What did you learn there? What does "Living Water" mean to you?

Clearly Jesus believes in you, now all you need is for you to believe in yourself.

AS YOU WANDER

91. Spoiler Alert

"No longer will there be any curse. The throne of God and of the Lamb will be in the city, and his servants will serve him. They will see his face, and his name will be on their foreheads. There will be no more night. They will not need the light of a lamp or the light of the sun, for the Lord God will give them light. And they will reign for ever and ever."
- Revelation 22:3-5 (NIV)

Everybody has that friend. The one who invites you over to watch a movie they've seen a million times. They sing the songs, repeat the lines, or ruin the ending of the story by slipping the plot before it even unwinds.

You're a little disgruntled because what's the point of even watching the movie if you already know the ending, right? Why get all caught up in the suspense or the romance if you know the main character survives and that couple ends up together? Well, I'm about to be that friend for you. Don't hate me, but I've read the last book of the Bible. Want to know what happens at the end of the story?

SPOILER ALERT- God wins! He restores all things. And, we, as believers, get to walk with Him in heaven and on this new earth forever.

Now that you know, you don't have to get caught up in living through the ups and downs of the crazy plot twists life will throw at you. You don't even have to think of the worst thing that could happen, start having FOMO, or inventing things to worry about. You can stop living like the ending is going to be bad or you're the victim when you know it's all good and, through Christ, you're the victor.

The final chapter of the Bible is God's Word for us all. "Trust me, it's going to be ok."

Journal or Doodle:

How is the ending of the Bible the best spoiler alert you've ever heard? What situation in your life do you find yourself believing that the outcome is going to be bad? Take a few moments to speak God's truth over that situation right now. How does your perspective change?

92. Hope Rises

"May the God of hope fill you with all joy and peace as you trust in him, so that you may overflow with hope by the power of the Holy Spirit."
- Romans 15:13 (NIV)

I lived in a mountain house in college that didn't have heat! Call us crazy, but my roommates and I really believed in space heaters and lower rent payments.

In Boone, North Carolina, it can get pretty chilly in the winter. How do you survive in negative five-degree wind chill on the second floor of a creaky old house? Simply turn on the space heater at the bottom of the stairs.

Heat rises. To warm up the top floor of any building, just get the bottom floor nice and toasty.

Hope actually works the same way.

Sometimes our circumstances seem cold or frozen. We cannot move because there is no clear direction. Nothing is working out. Our dreams are not coming true. The fire in us is going out.

However, when hope is the foundation of our lives, nothing can push down the joy and peace rising up in our hearts. Hope is the space heater thawing out the faith we need to move forward. It offers us the comfort we need to find contentment right where we are.

Journal or Doodle:

How can you let hope rise in your life, even when circumstances are trying to keep you down? What are the hopes and dreams that inspire you forward into your future?

93. When People See You

"And this will be a sign to you: You will find the baby wrapped in cloths and lying in a manger."
-Luke 2:12 (NIV)

When people see you, what do you think they see?

All your accolades or accomplishments? A potential success or failure? A social status or brand label?

When the angels first appeared to the shepherds in Matthew 2, the shepherds totally freaked out. So, to give credit to God's words the angels said, "And this will be a sign to you..."

Sometimes, like the shepherds, we need proof that we actually have a great part in God's story here on earth and that his Word is true for us. While Jesus isn't here any longer for us to go rush off with the shepherds to see lying in a manger, he is still present, living, and active here on earth. So, what's our sign that God's words are true?

You are.

Galatians 2:20 says that "*Christ... lives in you.*" Therefore, you are the focal point the angels now look to saying, *"Look, there's Jesus!" "Did you see the way she loved her friend? There's Jesus!" "Watch as they lead their generation to Truth. There's Jesus!" "Did you notice her hope in the hurt, joy in the pain, and integrity in the compromising situation? There's Jesus!"*

If you're seeking Jesus, try looking inside of you. Find Him there in your heart and shining in the lives of others who love Him. Live up to the high calling of being the sign someone is looking for.... that God is real and Jesus is here.

When people see you, do they see Jesus?

Journal or Doodle:

What do you think people see when they look at you? What do you want them to see? If you know someone who truly allows Jesus to live through them, what does that look like? If you have surrendered your life to Jesus, you are now living proof of God's love and presence here on the earth.

94. Chasing Shadows

"The people walking in darkness have seen a great light; on those living in the land of deep darkness a light has dawned."
-Matthew 4:16 (NIV)

If you ever watched Peter Pan as a kid, you'll remember that he was always chasing his shadow. It would fly away, hide, and even wrestle against him. Why did Peter want to catch his shadow?

Peter was probably looking for the same things we're all looking for, presence and purpose. To not have a shadow means you're not fully there or alive. Some great part of you is disconnected and missing. Sound familiar?

We all have our own Peter Pan moments and find ourselves frantically chasing after answers to the questions: Who am I really? How do I fully become who God meant for me to be?

When our sense of presence seems to be flying away from us, here are two ways we can hold our ground and connect to God's purpose for our lives.

1. Don't stand in someone else's shadow.
In the social media age, this is so incredibly hard. We're constantly bombarded by other people's highlight reels and wish so badly we could attach ourselves to that kind of life. We start grasping for things that don't actually reflect us at all. Social status, interests, clubs, brands, boys. All of the sudden, we find ourselves standing there wondering who we are.

Get out of the shadow of others and find your own shape and size. God made you to be you, not someone else.

2. Step into the light.
Just like we can't see a shadow unless there is light projecting onto an object, we can't really find ourselves until we step into the light of God's Word. We can go to scripture and prayer to ask God who he made us to be. If something doesn't line up with what He says through the Bible, it's a lie. Through scripture, we can claim these wonderful truths: we are beautiful, accepted, known, loved, chosen, forgiven and free.

Don't waste your time chasing shadows. Step into the light and find in God's Word the wild, wonderful woman you were designed to be.

<u>Journal or Doodle:</u>

What are some shadows you have chased as you've tried to discover your presence and purpose? Who does God's Word say you are? What unique attributes did He give you to impact the world around you?

95. Brokenness Is The Best

"But the seed falling on good soil refers to someone who hears the word and understands it. This is the one who produces a crop, yielding a hundred, sixty or thirty times what was sown."
-Matthew 13:23 (NIV)

With a kill count of two cactuses thus far in college, the phone conversation with my grandmother started out like this. *"I bought a real plant this time. A REAL thing that needs WATER and SUNLIGHT. How in the world do I keep this thing ALIVE!?"*

The first thing she told me about was soil. For anything to grow, the soil has to be good and broken. All of the sudden, I understood why our brokenness is the best thing that could ever happen to us.

In Matthew 13, Jesus shared a parable about seeds. Some fell on hard soil and were scattered. Others fell among thorns and were choked out. A few were planted but didn't sprout roots so they withered away. However, verse 23 says *"The seed that fell on good soil represents those who truly hear and understand God's word and produce a harvest of thirty, sixty or even a hundred times as much as had been planted!"*

The seed that fell on good, tilled, broken soil produced the harvest. Seeds not only grew, they multiplied!

When things come into our lives and break us apart, they're actually preparing us to grow. They're making our lives fertile soil to allow God to plant something deep into our hearts so that we produce great things.

Journal or Doodle:

Through your brokenness, what do you think God is preparing you for? What seed is growing in your heart?

96. Frailty Isn't Failure

"But we have this treasure in jars of clay to show that this all-surpassing power is from God and not from us."
-2 Corinthians 4:7 (NIV)

I had a hard conversation with my best friend yesterday. There were tears. I dumped out my struggles, insecurities, and weaknesses as if they were all that existed in me. After getting everything out that was stuffed inside, I felt relieved.

The next morning I was thinking about the talk and started to dwell on how weak I am. Why couldn't I be less emotional? Why can't I be superwoman? Why would I dump so much on my friend when half of everything I said was personal and had nothing to do with her? Do I even remember what I said? Pouring coffee into my mug, 2 Corinthians 4:7 came to mind and it made me stop beating myself up long enough to realize that we were all made to reach out.

As women, we tend to see our frailties as failures but God sees them as a necessity for fellowship.

Just as we need to open up to other people to digest our problems and find resolution, we need to open up to God. We can come to him saying, *"There is no lid on my jar, God. I'm cracked, broken, and empty. You are the pourer of living water, so fill me up. You are the potter, so fix me up."* It is in the confession of our weakness that we become stronger in God's power. We cannot fix or fill ourselves. We need Him to mold us in order to help us. He designed it that way.

My challenge for you is to become a generation of young women who stand up in a do-it-yourself culture and say that they are not self-made but God-made. That frailty isn't failure. It's actually through the need for empowerment from God's love and the support of others that we become fighters, a force to be reckoned with, and the change we wish to see in the world.

Journal or Doodle:

How can your weaknesses allow the opportunity for God and others to serve as your strength? What frailties have drawn you and your friends closer? Write down the name of a friend who may feel weak that you can support and encourage today.

97. Made To Thrive

"The thief comes only to steal and kill and destroy; I have come that they may have life, and have it to the full."
- John 10:10 (NIV)

You were made to thrive! I know that's hard to believe when typically days look like this:

Alarm. Class. Club or practice. Work. Homework. Eat. Sleep. Repeat. Blah, blah, blah...

We think that thriving should look like this:

Alarm. Crush coffee. Slay at school. Ace the test. Get elected as club president or employee of the month. Have a great hair day. Go out and grab a social media post worthy dinner with all your besties. Pass out into bed with no left over energy after the most successful day of your life. BAM!

The reality is that most days look average at best. We're surviving, not thriving. We're going through the motions, not witnessing miracles or having mountain top moments. Basically, we could walk out many of our days with our eyes closed.

However, we were meant to live eyes wide open. The true definition of thriving according to dictionary.com is this, *"grow or develop well or vigorously. Prosper; flourish."* So thriving isn't being a total boss at life, it's simply growing. It's seeing that the cup is half empty sometimes and asking God to pour out a little bit more.

While Satan may be trying to rob your joy and steal your passion for this life, John 10:10 says God is giving you days full of potential, promise, and opportunities to grow. Jesus didn't come so we could just survive; He came so that we could really live life. To the brim. Overflowing. If we will just make the choice today to thrive.

Journal or Doodle:

What do your days typically look like? How can you break out of survival mode and begin to thrive today?

98. The Camp High

"But whenever he entered the Lord's presence to speak with him, he removed the veil until he came out. And when he came out and told the Israelites what he had been commanded, they saw that his face was radiant. Then Moses would put the veil back over his face until he went in to speak with the Lord."
-Exodus 34: 34-35 (NIV)

"The camp high." Have you ever heard of it?

Basically it's Christianese for having an incredible, supernatural, spiritual experience with God. It's the best church camp you ever encountered. It's that retreat weekend and night you gave your life to Jesus. It's how you felt on that mission trip.

So, this could be an ordinary, mundane day. However, did you know that God is the same God that he was on the best weekend of your life? That you're still as connected to Him now as you were then? That he still wants to move in and through you in supernatural ways?

We can't chase "the camp high" because the true calling of our lives is to experience Jesus and then climb down off that mountaintop. We're to get in the valley where there's ordinary, hurt, and problems, then lift others up as high as we can.

We're to be like Moses, who encountered God so closely on Mount Sinai that when he came down off the mountain, his face shown with the glory of God. His encounter was evident.

Today, on an ordinary day, carry with you a memory of an extraordinary experience you've had with God.

Journal or Doodle:

If you've had a "camp high" experience, what was it like? How can you live out your "high" even in the lowest valleys of your life? How can you act toward others so that your encounter with Christ is evident?

99. What Is Worship Really?

"Now the earth was formless and empty, darkness
was over the surface of the deep, and the Spirit of God
was hovering over the waters."
-Genesis 1:2 (NIV)

When we think of worship, we think of God-Karaoke.
People with microphones. Lyrics on a screen.
Everyone singing along.

But, what is worship really?

Pastor and Founder of the Passion movement, Louie
Giglio, says, *"Worship is simply giving God His breath
back."*

The word for "Spirit" used in Genesis 1:2 is "ruah"
meaning "breath or wind."

I remember hearing a teaching in college on this
Hebrew word. "Ruah" is not just inhaling and exhaling.
It's more like breathing face-to-face with someone. It's
similar to a kiss or giving someone CPR.

This is what I want you to get: Worship is anything we
do to allow God to get in our face. It's an action that
allows us to give or receive life. It's really any gift or
talent we choose to give back to God in order that we
may grow closer.

Worship could be singing or playing an instrument on
a stage. However, it could also be playing a sport,
painting, making guacamole, fixing someone's hair for

a special event, writing on your blog, or taking friends on a favorite hike.

Take a moment to think about the Holy Spirit – He is with us and among us. He can come as close as we allow him to. So, whatever you do, worship today and let God get intimately near.

Journal or Doodle:

What does worship look like for you? What do you do that makes you come alive? What is assuring or uncomfortable about the thought of coming face-to-face with the Holy Spirit through worship?

100. Why Tribe?

"Let's see how inventive we can be in encouraging love and helping out, not avoiding worshiping together as some do but spurring each other on..."
-Hebrews 10:24-25 (MSG)

"As You Wander" was inspired out of the belief that comparison culture cannot exist when we're a community of women who celebrate one another. We can be lured back into authentic sisterhood by Jesus' love. We can lock arms with each other and support one another as we grow into women under the authority of God's Word.

So, why tribe? Or go to church? Join this Christian community? Make new friends?

Community is what stirs us to express God's goodness for the good of others. Sisterhood makes us aware, accountable and authentic.

Some may say, *"I don't have to go to church to be a Christian."* And, they're right. However, you do have to be connected to community to be encouraged in love and inspired forward into faith.

We thrive when we tribe because it's others that God uses to mold us into who we are.

Continue to connect with our online community on Instagram (@asyouwandertribe) and know the best part of your journey with Jesus has just begun. We're here cheering you on! Keep wandering.

Journal or Doodle:

What's your favorite thing about your friends, church and community? What have you learned about sisterhood from "As You Wander?" How will you remain studying God's Word and connecting with Christian community after completing this journal?

Wander always.
This is how we change
the world.

AS YOU WANDER

67516955R00120

Made in the USA
Columbia, SC
01 August 2019